COMFORT
AND
STRENGTH
IN THE
TIME OF
NEED

BILLY BEDFORD

COMFORT AND STRENGTH IN THE TIME OF NEED

iUniverse books may be ordered through booksellers or by contacting:

iUniverse
1663 Liberty Drive
Bloomington, IN 47403
www.iuniverse.com
844-349-9409

ISBN: 978-1-6632-3564-0 (sc)
ISBN: 978-1-6632-3578-7 (e)

Print information available on the last page.

iUniverse rev. date: 02/08/2022

This book is dedicated to my mother, Gwendolyn Louise Bedford who passed away on February 16, 2021. God used her and she was very inspirational with my drive toward the Lord.

SERMON TOPICS

WE MIGHT BE GROWN BUT WE ARE NOT OUR OWN

How well many of us have said or mumbled under our breath that I can't wait till I am grown. After becoming grown guess what? We are not our own we still have to answer to mankind we might be grown but the electric bill await us. House mortgage doesn't give us a pass on being grown. The PO PO 👮is going to let us know we are not our own 🚓. Most important is for us to know is that God says we are bought with a price (🩸) the 🩸of Jesus and are not our own. (1 Corinthians 7:23). You feel you are in a battle. But the battle is not yours it belongs to the Lord. (2 Chronicles 20:15). Because we are not our own we should not lean to our own understanding but trust in the Lord with all your heart and in all your ways acknowledge him and he will direct your path. (Proverbs 3:5). We are not our own therefore we are to render no one evil for evil. (Romans 12:17) Vengeance is mine says God I will repay (Romans 12:18).

WE ARE IN A FIGHT

In life we find ourselves in a fight. Job said a man/ mankind born of a woman is of few days and full of trouble. (Job 14:1). We can win the fight in spite of few days and full of trouble. How so Pastor? We can win the fight because God is our refuge and strength, a very present help in trouble. (Psalms 46:1). When you have trouble winning the fight and need help. Let's do what David said he did. I will lift my eyes 👀to the hills from where comes my help my help come from the Lord who made the heaven and earth. (Psalms 121:1). This fight is not against one another we are to win this fight and love one another. (John 13:35). Let's win this fight and not fight each other. For we wrestle not against flesh and blood, but against principalities, against powers, against rulers of darkness of this world and spiritual wickedness in high places. (Ephesians 6:12). This fight is not with a 9 millimeter, nor a case 🔪nor a 2 by 4 🔨. The weapons of our warfare are not carnal but mighty through God to the pulling down of strongholds. (2 Corinthians 10:4). We can win the fight because Jesus causes us to triumph. (2 Corinthians 2:14).

HE WAS HELD FOR ME, TO MAKE ME FREE

There are many things that would've/ could've/ should've happened to us. But God!! If it had not been the Lord who was on our side, we would have been swallowed up. (Psalms 124:1). We would have been consumed a long time ago. It was the Lord's mercies that we are not consumed because his compassions doesn't fail us. (Lamentations 3:22). It is all in the making of that he was held (on the cross) for you and for me that we could be free. The truth was held for you and me. What is truth? His word is truth. (John 17:17). It's good to know the truth. For you shall know the truth and the truth shall make you free. (John 8:32). When he was held he brought what grandma calls SHO Nuff !! For who the son (Jesus) sets free they are free indeed (Sho Nuff!!). (John 8:36). Isaiah the eagle eye Prophet saw one coming over 700 years before he came that would make/ set us free. Unto us a child is born unto us a son is given and the government shall be laid upon his shoulder. His name shall be called Wonderful, Counselor, The Mighty God, Everlasting Father, and the Prince of Peace. (Isaiah 9:6). He also saw what he was going to go through with in the process of set/ making us free. He was wounded for our transgressions, bruised for our iniquities, the chastisement of our peace was upon him and with his stripes we are healed. (Isaiah 53:5).

He Was Held for Me, To Make Me Free Part 2

May we be encouraged to know that Jesus Christ wants all mankind to be free. You shall know the truth and the truth shall make you free. Whoever the son (Jesus) sets free is free indeed. His way of making us free was to willingly lay down his life for us. He gave his life as a ransom for many. He shed his blood for the remission (removal) of our sins. He did it to save us from the wrath to come. He died for our sins that we all might have the right to the tree of life. They raised him up they stretched him WIDE. He hung his head and then he DIED. But that's not how the story ENDS, 3 days later he rose AGAIN.

I HEAR YOU & I SEE YOU: NOW YOU TAKE IT FROM THERE

I pray every heart be encouraged to know that the Lord hear us and that he sees all we go/going through. David said I waited patiently for the Lord; And he inclined to me and heard my cry. (Psalms 40:1). Since with God there is no respect of person (Romans 2:11). He hears us and he sees us. Mankind may not regard what things you do but God says no good thing will he withhold from them that walk upright. (Psalms 84:11). Mankind may forget about you. But God says I hear you daughter and I see you mother. He is not unrighteous to forget your work and labor of Love. (Hebrews 6:10). Keep doing the will of God for he hears you and he sees you. But Pastor I am tired of having my kindness taken for granted. Let us not be weary in well doing for you will reap in due season if you faint not. (Galatians 6:9). As a matter of fact mankind doesn't have to hear you or see you for you to be blessed. He says when you pray enter your secret closet and the Lord that see you in secret will reward you openly. When you give alms (Money, etc…) Don't let your left hand know what your right hand is doing. Give it in secret and thy Father which see in secret will reward you openly. Matthew 6:5-7)

I HEAR YOU & I SEE YOU: NOW YOU TAKE IT FROM THERE PART 2

God is omniscient (Knowing everything) The Bible says he declaring the end from the beginning. (Isaiah 46:10). The psalmist says Lord you have searched me, and known me. You know my down sitting and my uprisings, and understand my thoughts from afar. (Psalms 139:1-2). God is also Omnipresent (Everywhere at the same time. Where can I go from his spirit? Or where can I flee from his presence? If I ascend up into heaven, you are there: If I make my bed 🛏in hell 🔥, behold you are there. If I take the wings of the morning 🕊and dwell in the uttermost parts of the sea 🌊;even there your hand lead me and your right hand shall hold me. (Psalms 139:8-9). His eyes 👀are in every place looking at the evil and the good. (Proverbs 15:3). David said his eyes are upon the righteous and his ears 👂are open to their cry. (Psalms 34:15). This is Part one We should be rest assured that the Lord hears us and sees us. You may say why hasn't he moved in my life? God says my hand is not shortened that I cannot save, my ears 👂are not heavy 👂that I cannot hear. He said your sins have separated between you and your God. Your iniquities have hid his face that he will not hear. (Isaiah 59:1-2). Therefore we should out of a repentant heart call on him. You shall call me and I will answer you and show you things you know not of. (Jeremiah 33:3)

I Hear You & I See You: Now You Take It From There Part 3

Part 3: I hear you and I see you, now you take it from there. With the knowledge of knowing no matter what we been through/ going through the Lord hears 👂and sees 👀. We can/ should take it from there. 5 ways you and I can take it from there.

1. Have faith- Faith comes by hearing and hearing by the word of God.

2. Be confident- Being confident of this very thing. That he (Jesus) who has begun a good work in you will perform (Complete) it until the day of Jesus Christ. (Philippians 1:6).

3. What is formed to hurt/ destroy you WON'T. No weapon formed against you shall prosper. (Isaiah 54:17).

When you take it from there, you are not alone. I will never leave you or forsake you. (Hebrew 13:5).

4. If you are sick 🤒or have love ones you are concerned with their health and well being. He hears 👂you and he sees you. He is our healer. For there is a balm in Gilead. (Jeremiah 8:22) he is the great physician. He was wounded for our transgressions, bruised for our iniquities, the chastisement of our peace was upon him and with his stripes we are healed. (Isaiah 53:5).

5. He hears you and he sees you and doesn't want us to have fear. God has not given us a spirit of FEAR, but of POWER, LOVE, and a sound MIND!! (2 Timothy 1:7).

IT'S JESUS AND THAT'S MY FINAL ANSWER

One doesn't have to be a Bible theologian to know that Jesus is essential to our lives Spiritually, Physically, Mentally, economically.

Spiritual: Neither is there salvation in any other for there is no other name (Than Jesus) under heaven given among mankind whereby we may be saved. (Acts 4:12)

Physical: Peter and John told the lame man in the name of Jesus Christ of Nazareth, rise up and walk. (Acts 3:6).

Mentally: Jesus healed a man that hollered, and cut himself in a cemetery. Naked, could not be tamed. They found him later sitting, clothed, and in his right mind. (Mark 5:15).

Economically: Jesus said whatever you ask in my name. That will I do. (John 14:13).

IT'S JESUS AND THAT'S MY FINAL ANSWER PART 2

The context of this message is that they kept trying to get the man born blind to change his answer to who opened his eyes 👀. To his credit Jesus was always his final answer. If God has opened our eyes (Spiritual eyes 👀) we ought to make Jesus our final answer. Let the redeemed of the Lord say so who he has redeemed from the hand of the enemy. He should be the final answer through all and above all. God gave him a name highly exalted above every name (Above every sickness, disease, heavy burden, etc...) That at the name (Authority, character) of Jesus that every knee shall bow 🧎and every tongue 👅must confess that Jesus is Lord (he is master). When we make him the final answer his name becomes a strong tower the righteous run 🏃in and they are safe. I close by saying he has to be the final answer to get to the Father (I am the way the truth and the life) John 14:6

WHERE ARE YOU GOING; GOD IS NOT THROUGH WITH YOU

I remember my mom using these words when verbally chastising me (where are you going, I am not through with you) Likewise With the Lord I have been wanting to go on before the Lord was through with me. Paul urged in Philippians to be confident of this very thing, that he (Jesus) which has begun a good work in us will perform it (complete it) until the day of Jesus Christ. He is not through with us, He will show us great and mighty things which we know not of. He is not through with us, he can/ will do for us. He is able to do exceedingly, abundantly above all that we can ask or think. He is not through with us he has things in store for us. Eye 👁hath not seen nor ear 👂heard neither has it entered in the heart ♥of man, what the Lord has prepared for them that love him.

A Place For You Both
Now & Later

I remember as a child eating a candy ⊁⊱called NOW & Later eat some now save some for later). I come to find that God has a place for us both Now & Later) We can enjoy some now and enjoy some later. When we forsake all for the Kingdom sake we will receive (NOW) manifold blessings. And in the world ⊕to come (LATER) everlasting life. He will withhold (NOW) no good thing from them that walk up rightly. He has prepared (NOW) a house of many mansions for us. And where he is (NOW) There we will be also (LATER).

Don't Fret it, Don't Sweat It, Give It To Jesus And You Won't Regret It

The Bible says FRET (Be constantly and visibly worried or anxious) not yourselves because of evil doers. (Psalms 37:1). Nor should we ☺sweat the things we face in life. In life we will have tribulations but be of good cheer for I have overcome the world. We should give it Jesus and we want regret that we did. David said I was young but now am old yet have I never seen the righteous forsaken nor their seed begging bread. Psalms 37:25).

I Thought I Saw A Way Out, I Did See A Way Out Part 2

Our subject title today reminds me of the tweetie bird that said I thought I saw a putty cat, then said I did I did saw a putty cat. If you thought through Jesus Christ you saw a way out then you did. Sometimes for a way out he calls us out of darkness into this marvelous light. Sometimes he tells us the way out. He told Thomas I am the way the truth and the life. He said in John that I am the door of the sheep by me if anyone enters they will be saved. He is the way to the father. No one comes to the father but by me. He is the way out when trouble arises. He is our refuge and strength a very present help in trouble. What and how we think is important. So as one think so are they. May we all look to Jesus the author and finisher of our faith. May we all lift our eyes to the hills from where our help comes.

It Is Coming, You Just Stay The Course!

In life it is important that we stay the course (route or direction). The race is not given to the swift or the strong but to the one that endure (continue, persevere, last) to the end. We are told to lay aside every weight and sin which easily beset us, and let us run this race with patience which is set before us. Looking unto Jesus the author and finisher (perfector) of our faith. We are encouraged to not be weary in well doing for in due season we shall reap if we faint not. Paul said therefore my beloved brethren be steadfast, unmovable always abiding in the work of the Lord for as much as we know that your labor is not in vain.

WHEN I CAME TO MYSELF

Before I came to myself I was like burger ⊜king motto: HAVE IT YOUR WAY. When I came to myself I now know that my way is not his way (God) and my thoughts 💭are not his thoughts. I was like Paul, when I was a child 😊I thought 💭as a child, spake as a child, did childish things. When I became a man (when I came to myself) I put away childish things. We perhaps can relate to the prodigal (lost) son. We came to ourselves and realized what we have with Abba father. We have in him Peace that surpasses all understanding. Joy unspeakable and full of glory. Life and life more abundantly. We have the gift of God (which is ETERNAL LIFE.)

THIS IS WHAT I CAME
TO DO FOR YOU

This is a faithful saying and worthy of all acceptance that Christ Jesus came into the world ✸to save sinners (1 Timothy 1:15). The angels told Joseph that she (Mary) was going to bring forth a son, and they would call his name Jesus for he shall save his people from their sins. Luke said that the son of man (Jesus) come to seek and to save that which is lost. He commend his love toward us, in that while we were sinners Christ died for us. He also came to save us from the wrath to come. May we all allow him to do what he came to do for us ♥🙏.

LET'S FOCUS ON THE PROMISE

We are not exempt from problems, for a man/mankind born of a woman is of few days and full of trouble. We should not let the problem be our focus, we should focus on the promise. When we focus on the promise we won't be weary in well doing for he promised in due season we shall reap if we faint not. When we focus on the promise we can count it all joy when we fall into different temptations. When we focus on the promise we can forget those things that are behind and reach forth to what is before us, and press towards the mark of the high calling of God which is in Christ Jesus. It has much to do with how we think 😕💭. So a man thinks 😕 💭, so is he. Be encouraged to keep your mind Christ like. Let (allow) this mind be in you which was also in Christ Jesus. He will keep those in perfect (complete) peace whose mind is stayed on him. Let's not focus on the PROBLEM let's focus on the PROMISE. Please share this message with others for many are going through problems that God has great promises prepared for them.

A Hope That Is Built On Nothing Less Than Jesus Christ And His Righteousness

When one builds his house on a solid foundation (they are likened unto a wise person. Therefore it will be wise of us to build on nothing less than Jesus Christ. I say this because without him (Jesus) we could do nothing. Our hope should not be built upon things (money 💵, cars 🚗,etc...) which will perish with the using there of. If in this life only we have hope, we are of all men/ mankind most miserable. Yes we have need of things in which God knows what we have need of even before we ask. When our hope is built on him we prioritize by seeking first the Kingdom of God and his righteousness and all these things (money 💵cars 🚗, etc...) will be added to us. Hope built on Jesus sets their affection on things above and not on things of the earth. Where our treasures are that's where our hearts are. We thank God for the blessed hope JESUS CHRIST!!

LEAN ON IT

Jesus said he will never leave us or forsake us. He said he will be with us even to the end of the world. As a matter of fact his name shall be called Emmanuel (which being interpreted means God with us). Paul said if God be for us who can be against us? If you are in trouble right now, you can lean on Jesus, for he is a very present help in time of trouble. When the enemy comes in like a flood, the spirit of the Lord will lift up a standard against him. Jesus said to Peter that satan desires to have you and sift you as wheat 🌾, but I have prayed 🙏for you that your faith fail you not. Lean on him if it's sickness, for by his stripes we are healed. Lean on him when the MONEY 💵is FUNNY 😖, when the CHANGE is STRANGE, and when your CREDIT can't GET IT. Our God shall supply all of your needs according to his riches in Glory by Christ Jesus. Please share with others for many are in need of someone to lean on.

Lean on It Part 2

Jesus desires that we lean on him and not to our own understanding but to trust him with all our heart, acknowledge him in all our ways and he will direct our path. He is a friend that sticks closer than any brother. He is one that love us at all times. Be encouraged my brethren to cast (throw) all your cares (anxieties, burdens, etc..) upon him for he cares for you. He paid the ultimate price for us, he shed his blood. Without the shedding of blood there would be no remission (removal)of our sins. He died for our sins that we might have the right to the tree of life. He rose again from the grave the third day according to the scriptures. When we lean on him no man can pluck you out of his hand. When we lean on him nothing shall be able to separate us from the love of God. Lean on him and no weapon formed against you shall prosper. Lean on him and you will testify that greater is he that is within you than he that is in the world. I pray all be encouraged to lean on Jesus the more. I ask that you click on link and share with others. May God bless you 🙏.

Moving With A Sense of Urgency

This sermon is about Jonas . We often depict him as one that procrastinated to the call of God. God told him to go to Nineveh but he went to Joppa to get to Tarshish away from the presence of the Lord (Jonah 1:1). Before we judge Jonah let's remember that we ourselves were sometimes foolish and disobedient. (Titus 3:3). Perhaps went against his will and did what he said not to do such as lean not to your own understanding but trust in the Lord with all your heart and acknowledge him in all your ways and he will direct your path. (Proverbs 3:5) Thank God that he is a God of another chance. If we confess our sins God is faithful and just to forgive us our sin and the blood ♦of his son Jesus will cleanse us from all unrighteousness. (1 John 1.9). When God came to Jonah a second time he obeyed God and moved with a sense of urgency. The journey to Nineveh was a 3 days journey. Jonah made the Journey in 1 day!!. I hear Jesus saying I must be about my father's business (Luke 2:49). I hear Jesus saying I must work the works of him that has sent me while it is day, for the night comes when no one can work. (John 9:4).

LETS NOT FOCUS ON OUR BEEN THROUGH, LET'S FOCUS ON OUR BREAKTHROUGH

Sermon Title: Let's not focus on our been through, let's focus on our breakthrough. Many that are reading this topic have been through so much, that you cannot deny I admonish you to focus on your breakthrough. Your been through has caused you to 😔. Your breakthrough is coming for they that sow in tears 😭shall reap in Joy (Psalms 126:5). Weeping may endure for a night but Joy comes in the morning (Psalms 30:5). You been through things in which your kindness was taken for granted. Your breakthrough is coming. Let us not be weary in well doing for in due season we shall reap if we faint not. (Galatians 6:9). You have been waiting on a breakthrough, Your breakthrough is coming. They that wait upon the Lord he shall renew their strength, they shall mount up with wings as eagles 🦅. You shall run 🏃and not get weary. You shall walk and not faint. (Isaiah 28:31).

SOONER OR LATER IT WILL WORK IN YOUR FAVOR

In a life with Jesus Christ things have a way of working itself out. He causes us to always triumph (Come out victorious). I admonish you to be confident that Jesus has begun a good work in you and he will complete it until the day of Jesus Christ. When doing good and your kindness is taken for granted, don't be weary in your well doing for in due season (at the appropriate time) you are going to reap if you faint not. You have been through so many things, be encouraged to know that all things (everything you been through and are going through) work together for the good of them who love the Lord and are the called according to his purpose).

COME CLOSER WHERE YOU CAN SEE ME BETTER

Sermon Title: Come closer, where you can see me better! The Lord doesn't have to come closer to see us better for he is Omnipresent (Everywhere) The eyes 👀of the Lord is in every place beholding (looking) the evil and the good. (Proverbs 15:3). He is looking at us desiring for us to come closer to him. His eyes 👀are upon the righteous and his ears 👂are open to their cry. (Psalms 34:15). Therefore he says to you and I draw near (close) to God and he will draw near to us. (James 4:8). It is vital that we come closer. Jesus told Nicodemus except a man be born again he cannot SEE the Kingdom of God. (John 3:5). Everyone that came closer to him. There was a time that they weren't so close. Paul said when I was a child I spoke as a child, I thought 💭as a child, I did childish things, but when I became a man (came closer) I put away childish things. (1 Corinthians 13:11). Truth be told we all stand in need of coming closer to him. We need the truth spoken to us. We as Pastors should tell the truth when preaching the Gospel. Paul told Timothy to be instant (and Ready) in season (When they want to hear it) and out of season (when that don't want to hear it. (2 Timothy 4:2)

JESUS WILL MAKE STRAIGHT THE MOTHERS AND ALL THE OTHERS

Happy Mother's Day ♥🙏. Sermon Title: Jesus will make it it straight for the MOTHERS and all the OTHERS!! To make straight means to fix or make right. What has been done to the mothers he will make it RIGHT!! All your battles he will FIGHT. There's a mansion in the sky he will DEED you. Off the fatness of the land he will FEED you. And the high places he will bring down for you.

In You And In Me Is Where He Wants To Be

Sermon Title: In YOU and in ME is where he wants to be. Part 2: There is no better place for Christ to be than in us. Paul said to the church at Corinth examine yourselves as to whether you be in the faith. Prove your own selves don't you know your own selves that Christ is in you except you be reprobates (Rejected) (2 Corinthians 13:5). He has to be in you for you to exemplify the fruits of the spirit (Love, Joy, Peace, etc... 6 more) (Galatians 5:22). On the other hand if anyone have not his spirit then he is none of his (Romans 8:9). When he is in you no weapon formed against you shall prosper (Isaiah 54:17). When he is in you the enemy shall come in like a flood but the spirit of the Lord will lift up a standard against him (Isaiah 59:19). Satan the prince of this world/ system (John 16:11) is on your track trying to turn you back. I am here to encourage you and let you know that greater is he that is in you (Jesus) than he that is in the world (Satan)(1 John 4:4). When Christ is in you that means he is for you. If God be for us who can be against us? (Romans 8:28-31). It is essential that he be where he want to be and that in in YOU and in ME!!

WITH OUR HEARTS FILLED WITH LOVE HE WILL WRITE OUR NAMES ABOVE

Sermon title: With our hearts filled with LOVE he will write 📖our names ABOVE!! One of the most important things we should desire/ strive for is that the Lord has our name written in the lambs book of life. There shall in no wise (case) enter into it that defileth, neither whatsoever work abomination or make the a lie. But they that are written in the book 📖 of life. (Revelation 21:27). What gets us in the book will not be our work of righteousness. Not by works of righteousness that you have done are you saved, but by the washing and renewing and regeneration of the Holy Ghost (Titus 3:5). Our names are not written above by our good deeds. For by grace are you saved, not by works not of yourself lest anyone would boast it is the gift of God. (Ephesians 2:9). Demons are subject to us but that not why we should rejoice. We should rejoice because our names are written above. (Luke 10:20).

THE DEVIL IS A LIAR AND A DECEIVER TOO

Sermon title: The devil is a liar and a deceiver too, God is not through blessing you. Two of satan's main things that he uses is lies and deception. The Bible says he is a sinner from the beginning. (1 John 3:8). He was a murderer from the beginning and abode not in the truth. (John 8:44). He is also a deceiver of many. Insomuch he would deceive the very elect if it were possible. (Matthew 24:24). He will try to get you to deny the very Lord God that brought you. (2 Peter 2:1). He lied ☯and deceived Adam and Eve and has been a liar ☯and a deceiver ever since. But God is not through blessing you

SOME HOW SOME WAY THINGS ARE GOING TO WORK OUT OKAY

Sermon title: Some how some WAY, things are going to work out OKAY. By experience and study ▭of God word I can concur that things are going to work out okay. I have come to an understanding that many are the afflictions of the righteous. But it's going to be ok. Why because God will deliver you/ us out of them all. (Psalms 34:19). Job said a person born of a woman is of few days and full of trouble. (Job 14:1). You may say how then can everything be ok with few days and lots of trouble? I am glad you asked. It is going to be ok because God is our refuge and our strength, a very present help in trouble. Psalms 46:1). It's going to be ok if we by faith lift our eyes 👀to the hills from where comes our help. (Psalms 121:1). If we do our part. The lord said no good thing will he withhold from them that walk uprightly. (Psalms 84:11). David's testimony was I was young but now am old and I have never seen the righteous forsaken or his seed begging bread. (Psalms 37:25). The 3 Hebrew men's testimony was . The God we serve is able to deliver us out of the burning 🔥fiery furnace. (Daniel 3:17). Paul testimony was At my first answer no one stood with me. But the Lord stood by me. (2 Timothy 4:16).

A RACE THAT WE ALL CAN WIN

Sermon Title: A race we all can win part 2-I would be remiss (lack of duty) If I didn't say that there are some essentials (Necessities) on our behalf to win the Christian race. Oh how so brother Pastor?

1. You must be born again. Jesus told Nicodemus that except a man/mankind be born again they shall not enter the Kingdom of God. (John 3:5).

2. Your life will change. Therefore if anyone be in Christ they are a new creature, old things are passed away and behind all things are become new. (2 Corinthians 5:17)

3. Winners of the race are disciples (Follower/learner of God. If anyone will be his disciple let them deny themselves, take up their cross and follow him (Jesus) (Matthew 16:24).

4- Be filled (be controlled by) with the Holy Ghost. Peter said to them that were pricked in their heart and said men and brethren what must we do? Peter said Repent (Become Godly sorrow) for your sins. Be Baptized (Immersed in water) In the name (Character, Authority) Lord Jesus Christ1 Peter 1:16) for the remissions (removal) of your sins and you shall receive the Gift of the Holy Ghost. (Acts 2:38).

5. Winners strive to live Holy. Be Holy in all manner of conversation (conduct) Be ye Holy for I am Holy (Set aside for the master's use).

WITH GOD THERE IS JUSTICE

Father God in Jesus name I pray that every eye that view this message take confidence in knowing that there is Justice with you. The battle is not ours but belong to you. We should not pay anyone evil for evil. Moses said an 👁for an 👁and a 🦷for a 🦷. Jesus said Love your enemies. He said vengeance belongs to him and he will repay.

IF YOU KNOCK KNOCK ME DOWN I WILL GET BACK UP AGAIN

The Bible says a just man (righteous man) shall fall 7 times, and rise up again. (Proverbs 24:16). So though things may come against us we like Maya Angelou still we rise. We get back up because we are more than a conqueror through him (Jesus) that love us. (Romans 8:37). The enemy will come to knock you down but you can get back up again. For when the enemy comes in like a flood, the spirit of the Lord will lift up a standard against him. (Isaiah 59:19). Not that he won/t form (use) things against you. But there is no weapon that is formed against you that will prosper. (Isaiah 54:17). The way to get back up is to know that Greater is he (Jesus) that is within you than he that is in the world. (1 John 4:4). God has promised us to never leave us or forsake us. (Hebrews 13:5). He said I will be with you always even to the end of the world. (Matthew 28:20). In my closing I hear David saying I was young and now am old yet have I never seen the righteous forsaken nor their seed begging bread. (Psalms 37:25). If it Knock ✊Knock ✊me down. I will get back up again.

FOR PROPER REST, LET THE POWER OF CHRIST REST ON YOU

We need proper (The right kind of) rest both natural and spiritual. I wish above all that you mayest prosper and be in health as your soul prospers. (3 John 1:2). The proper way to do that is to allow the power of Christ to rest upon us. One way to get proper rest is to go to him. Come unto me all that labor and are heavy laden and I will give you rest (Matthew 11:28). For proper rest what we don't want to do is to do it as if we going to burger 🍔👑. We are not going to have it our way for our thoughts and our ways are not his ways and thoughts as a matter of fact Isaiah said it's as far away as the heaven is from the earth. (Isaiah 55:8). We should do as Matthew said and seek first the kingdom of God and his righteousness and all these things will be added unto you (Matthew 6:33). When the power of Christ rest upon us. No weapon 🔫 that is formed against you will prosper (Isaiah 54:17). When the power of Christ rest upon you. You can count it all joy when you fall into divers (Different temptations) James 1:1. When the power of Christ rest upon you. You can do all things through Christ who strengthens you. (Philippians 4:13). When the power of Christ rest upon you. Our God will supply all your needs according to his riches in glory by Christ Jesus. (Philippians 4:19).

FOR PROPER REST, LET THE POWER OF CHRIST REST ON YOU PART 2

Proper rest is the context of this message. Rest means to relax, recover oneself, or receive strength. We need rest both physically and spiritually. Proper rest is the right kind of rest (According to the scriptures). 5 ways to have proper rest.

A. Rest in the Lord and wait patiently for him. (Psalms 37:7)

B. Come to him when you need proper rest. Come to me all who labor and are heavy laden and I will give you rest. (Matthew 11:28)

C. Find a day and time to rest. Six days you shall work, but on the seventh day you shall rest in harvest you shall rest.

D. Be rest assured that God in the end will grant you proper rest. The wicked shall cease from troubling the righteous and the weary shall be at rest. (Job 3:17)

E. You will reap for your waiting patiently for him. Let us not be weary in well doing for we shall reap in due season if we faint not. (Galatians 6:9).

In my closing I hear Isaiah asking Have you not known? Have you not heard? That the everlasting God the Lord the creator of the earth faint not neither is he weary there is no searching of his understanding. He gives power to the faint and to them that have no might he increase their strength. Even the youth shall faint and be weary young men shall utterly fall, but they that wait upon the Lord he shall renew their strength they shall run and not be weary they shall walk and not faint. (Isaiah 40:28-31)

CALL ON THE ONE THAT CAN GET IT DONE PART 2

Call on the ONE that can get it DONE part 2: Part 1 should leave us no doubt that Jesus is the ONE that can get it DONE!! The odds may seem insurmountable but with God all things are possible. (Matthew 19:26). We need to trust him when we can't trace him. Lean not to your own understanding but TRUST in the Lord in all your ways acknowledge him and he shall direct your path (Proverbs 3:5). Believe he can get it done even if you can't see 👀it. For we walk by faith and not by SIGHT 👀. (2 Corinthians 5:7). Your MONEY 💵may be FUNNY😄, your CHANGE may be STRANGE and your CREDIT💳 can't GET IT. If we be like as the Philippians, Our God shall/ will supply all our needs according to his riches in Glory by Christ Jesus (Philippians 4:19). My brothers and sisters we serve a God that is as grandma said he is ABLE to put food 🍽(natural and spiritual) on your TABLE. He will give you Joy 😃in SORROW ☹, hope for TOMORROW. Weeping may endure for a night, but Joy comes in the morning. (Psalms 30:5). I say in my late Daddy's voice (Pastor Billy Gene Bedford) Ain't God is alright!! He is alright in the fact that he is ABLE to keep you from falling. (Jude 1:24). He is ABLE to save to the uttermost. (Hebrews 7:25). He is ABLE to do exceedingly, abundantly above all that we ask or think 🤔💭, according to the power that work within us (Ephesians 3:20).

Let's Wash Our Hands
It's Time To Eat

Scripture Matthew 27:17-29

Subject: Let's wash our hands it's time to eat!!

I use to love to hear the latter part of this message (It's time to eat). My mother put emphasis on washing your hands first. Spiritually we love to eat. We want the windows of heaven opened for us (Malachi 3:10). We love to have all our beds supplied (Philippians 3:19) We love to have his blessings to come upon us (Deuteronomy 28:1-14). Just like mom says you got to wash your hands God says we need our hands washed in other words we must allow God to change us. Therefore if anyone be in Christ they are a be creature old things are passed away and behold all things become new. (2 Corinthians 5:17). When we wash our hands we can benefit by submitting ourselves to God resist the devil and he will flee from us. (James 4:7). There are some things God require from us. You must be born again (John 3:5). Thankful that we serve a God that is merciful or we would be in trouble. His mercy is everlasting. (Psalms 100:5).

WHEN THE POTTER GETS IN THE HOUSE PART 2

PART 2: Reasons and purpose that the Potter (Jesus) desire to live in our house (Our bodies)

1.Why? Jesus came into this world to save sinners (You and I were born in sin and shaped in iniquity). 1 Timothy 1:15) He also came to seek and to save that which is lost (Luke 19:10)

2.How? Through the Virgin Mary. She shall bring forth a son and they shall call his name Jesus and he will save his people from their sin. (Matthew 1:21).

3.When? TODAY if you will hear his voice harden not your heart (Hebrews 3:8) And NOW is the accepted time (2 Corinthians 6:2).

4. What is going to happen? After the Holy Ghost has come upon you you shall have power. (Acts 1:8).

5. Where will I be when let the potter in my house.? Let not your heart be troubled if you believe in God believe also in me. For in my father's house there are many mansions if it was not so I would have told you. I go to prepare a place for you and if I go and prepare a place for you. I will come again and receive you unto myself that where I am there you may be also and where I go you will know and the way you will know. Thomas said to him Lord we don't know where you are going and how can we know the way? Jesus said to him I am the way the truth and the life and no one comes to the father but by me. (John 14:1-6).

LIFE LIBERTY AND THE PURSUIT OF HAPPINESS FOR ALL

This is a well known phrase given by the declaration of independence that the declaration says is given to all humans by their creator and protected by the government's that all have the unalienable rights to LIFE, LIBERTY, and the PURSUIT OF HAPPINESS. From experience and study of God 📖. That in order to have True life, liberty and pursuit of Happiness is going to come from the Lord. The constitution states that we hold these truths to be self evident that all mankind are created equal. There are many reading right now that have not been treated justly. In spite of you going beyond the call of duty I encourage you to not be weary in well doing for in due season you shall reap if you faint not (Galatians 6:9). You have considered taking matters in your own hands but I admonish you to avenge not yourselves for vengeance is mine I will repay saith the Lord. (Romans 12:18). The world system has caused you to lose confidence in many ways. I say to you cast not away (Don't throw away) your confidence for it has a great recompense of reward. (Hebrews 10:35). He didn't bring you this far to leave you without life liberty and the pursuit of Happiness. Be confident of this very thing, that he (Jesus) who has begun a good work in you he will perform (COMPLETE) it until the day of Jesus Christ (Philippians 1:6). In part 2 we shall give points as to how to have LIFE, LIBERTY AND THE PURSUIT OF HAPPINESS. In the meantime count it all joy when you fall into diverse (different) temptations. (James 1:2). It will get challenging but he promised to never leave you or forsake you. (Hebrews 13:5). For he told his disciples that I will be with you always even to the end of the world. (Matthew 28:20). David said I was young but now old, yet have I never seen the righteous forsaken or his seed begging 📖. (Psalms 37:25)

DON'T TAKE IT TO THE GRAVE, USE WHAT HE GAVE

The Lord blesses us with talents and gifts and he desire/require that we use them. In the parable of the pounds the one that had 1lb wrapped it in a Napkin and there were consequences. (Luke 19:20-27). When should we use our Talents? ANSWER: Remember NOW your creator (The Lord) in the days of your youth. (Ecclesiastes 12:1). Let us not take what he gave us to the GRAVE. Jesus said I must work the works he has sent me we while it is day, the night comes when no one can work. (John 9:4). At the age of 12 Jesus said to Mary and Joseph, I must be about my father's business. (Luke 2:49). I admonish you to use what he GAVE and not take it to the GRAVE.

LET US LOOK IN THE MIRROR, WE MIGHT NEED A FAITH LIFT

On the natural side of life one looks in the mirror to see if something needs putting on or pulling off. God desire us to look in the mirror of his word☐☐,in doing so we might find that we have all sinned and come short of the glory of God. (Romans 3:23). We along with many other bible patriarchs might find we need a FAITH lift. When the disciples could not do anything with the father whose son had a lunatic spirit Jesus asked them. How is it that you have no faith? (Mark 4:40). When Jesus told the apostles that if their brother trespassed against them 7 times in a day that they are to forgive him. They replied back Lord increase our faith. (Luke 17:5). When Jesus told the disciples that a rich man would not be easy for a rich man to enter the Kingdom of God. They asked him who then can be saved. So we are in good company if we need a FAITH LIFT. IN PART 2: We shall cover ways in which to obtain a FAITH LIFT.

It Will Come Out In The Wash

Our elderly use to say these words (It will all come out in the wash) They we're saying that things will work itself out and truly it will. The Bible says Be not deceived for God is not mocked, whatsoever a man/ person sows that shall they also reap (Galatians 6:7) Your giving will come out in the wash. Give and it shall be given unto you good measure, pressed down, shaken together and running over shall mankind give unto bosom for what measure you mete shall be mete back unto you. (Luke 6:38). Your mercy toward others will come out in the wash. Blessed are the merciful for they shall obtain mercy. (Matthew 5:7). What you sow to your flesh will come out in the wash. What you sow to your spirit will come out in the wash. If you sow to the flesh you will reap corruption. If you sow to the spirit you will reap life everlasting. (Galatians 6:8). If you don't give up in your well doing it will come out in the wash. Let us not be weary in well doing for we shall reap in due season if we faint not. (Galatians 6:9) Be encouraged to know that what you are going through although you do not understand. It's going to come out in the wash. We know that all things work together to the good of them that love God, to them that are the called according to his purpose. (Romans 8:28).

WITH OUR HEARTS FILLED WITH LOVE HE WILL WRITE OUR NAMES ABOVE

Sermon title: With our hearts filled with LOVE he will write our names ABOVE!! One of the most important things we should desire/ strive for is that the Lord has our name written in the lambs book of life. There shall in no wise (case) enter into it that defileth, neither whatsoever work abomination or make them a lie. But they that are written in the book of life. (Revelation 21:27). What get us in the book will not be our work of righteousness. Not by works of righteousness that you have done are you saved, but by the washing and renewing and regeneration of the Holy Ghost (Titus 3:5). Our names are not written above by our good deeds. For by grace are you saved, not by works not of yourself lest anyone would boast it is the gift of God. (Ephesians 2:9). Demons are subject to us but that not why we should rejoice. We should rejoice because our names are written above (Luke 10:20).

SOME HOW SOME WAY, THINGS ARE GOING TO WORK OUT OKAY

Sermon title: Some how some WAY, things are going to work out OKAY. By experience and study 📖of God word I can concur that things are going to work out okay. I have come to an understanding that many are the afflictions of the righteous. But it's going to be ok. Why because God will deliver you/ us out of them all. (Psalms 34:19). Job said a person born of a woman is of few days and full of trouble. (Job 14:1). You may say how then can everything be ok with few days and lots of trouble? I am glad you asked. It is going to be ok because God is our refuge and our strength, a very present help in trouble. (Psalms 46:1). It's going to be ok if we by faith lift our eyes 👀to the hills from where comes our help. (Psalms 121:1). If we do our part. The lord said no good thing will he withhold from them that walk uprightly. (Psalms 84:11). David testimony was I was young but now am old and I have never seen the righteous forsaken or his seed begging bread. (Psalms 37:25. The 3 Hebrew men testimony was: The God we serve is able to deliver us out of the burning 🔥fiery furnace. (Daniel 3:17). Paul testimony was: At my first answer no one stood with me. But the Lord stood by me. (2 Timothy 4:16).

No Ifs, Ands, Buts, Or Might: Let Us Get The Gospel Right

No ifs ands or buts or might part 2-In part one we covered some must facts in regards to us from the Lord. For example God is a spirit, and he seek such to worship him for they that worship him MUST WORSHIP him in spirit and in truth. (John 4:24). Thank God for his new mercies every morning. (Lamentations 3:23). Therefore we can all get the Gospel right. 5 Points as to how we can get the Gospel right.

POINT 1: STUDY ▢▢the word to show yourselves approved unto God a workman that need not to be ashamed rightly dividing the word of truth (2 Timothy 2:15).

POINT 2- DENY YOURSELF. Then said Jesus to his disciples, if anyone will come after me, let them deny themselves, and take up his cross and follow me. (Matthew 16:24).

POINT 3- BE FILLED WITH the HOLY GHOST. You shall receive power after the Holy ghost has come upon you (Acts 1:8).

POINT 4- BE A DOER OF THE WORD. BE DOERS OF the word and not hearers only. (James 1:22).

Point 5 Be a new creation in Christ Jesus. If anyone be in Christ they are a new creation, old things are passed away and behold all things are become new. (2 Corinthians 5:17).

As You Pick And Choose, Know That With The LORD There is No Way You Can Lose

In our natural life and spiritual life we will pick and choose. We sometimes choose according to our liking our liking can cause us to pick a problem. Case in point is Samson he chose Delilah and it cost him dearly. (Judges 16:1-13). We may choose according to our thoughts not always a good idea. Your thoughts are not his thoughts neither your ways his ways. (Isaiah 55:8). When we pick and choose we should lean not to our own understanding but trust in the Lord with all our hearts, and in all our ways acknowledge him and he will direct our path. (Proverbs 3:5). I know your choice may seem like the right choice but please understand that there is a way that seems right but the end thereof are the ways of death. (Proverbs 14:12). We all have made bad choices in life. How do you know that Pastor? Answer: All have sinned and come short of the glory of God. (Romans 3:23). Grandmother said when we know better we ought to do better. Paul made bad choices he said when I was a child I thought as a child, spoke as a child, did childish things but when I became a man I put away childish things. (1 Corinthians 13:11). My prayer is that we pick and choose according not to our will but let his will be done. (Matthew 26:42).

FOR THE RIGHT OUTCOME GET IN TOUCH WITH JESUS

Please click and enjoy a snippet of Rance Allen (Something about that name Jesus). As we look at Part 2 : Get in touch with Jesus. The woman with an issue of blood for 12 years had gotten in touch with many physicians and was not healed of any. She spent all she had and got no better but rather grew worse. She then got in touch with Jesus and said if I can touch the border/hem of his garment I will be made whole. I am here to tell you that Jesus told her that her faith had made her whole (Complete) Luke 8: 38-48). We too can get in touch with Jesus. There is no respect of persons with God. (Romans 2:11). How can we get in touch with Jesus? He said when you call me then I will answer when you call me I will say here I am. (Isaiah 58:9). How can I get in touch with Jesus? By faith (Romans 10:17) faith comes by hearing and hearing by the word of God. I want to get in touch with Jesus but I just don't see it happening for me. We don't go by what we see. We walk by faith and not by sight. (2 Corinthians 5:7). How do I get in touch with Jesus? Believe it. All things are possible to them that believe. (Mark 9:23) Even me Pastor? It can be you. David said I was a young man 😊but now am old yet have I never seen the righteous forsaken or their seed begging for bread. (Psalms 37:25).

STAY CONNECTED TO THE VINE AND YOU WILL BE JUST FINE

We are living in a time when much around us is not fine. Job said those that are born of a woman is of few days and full of trouble. (Job 14:1). Paul said in the last days perilous times will come. (2 Timothy 3:1) Jesus said in the end time you will hear of wars and rumors of wars. (Matthew 24:6). How then can we be just fine? I am glad you asked. We will be just fine by staying connected to the VINE. Jesus said I am the true vine. (John 15:1). Let's stay connected and be rest assured you will be fine. No good thing will he withhold from them that walk uprightly. (Psalms 84:11). Abide (Remain) in me and my word in you. You can ask what you will and it shall be done. (John 15:7). Stay connected to Jesus and he said whatever you ask in my name that will I do. (John 14:13). Stay connected and I will show you great and mighty things you know not of (Jeremiah 33:3).

STAY CONNECTED TO THE VINE AND YOU WILL BE JUST FINE PART 2

Stay connected part 2- On the natural side of life in order for things we use such as appliances to continue to work alright, they must stay connected to a power source. Likewise we must stay connected to our POWER SOURCE (Jesus Christ) He told his disciples that he is the true vine and if we abide (Remain connected) in him and his word in you that you can ask what you will and it shall be done. (John 15:7). We are the branch and the branch cannot do nothing of itself for Jesus said that without me you can do nothing. (John 15:5). Many feel their money will propel them without being connected. I heard the Bible say what shall it profit a man to gain the whole world and lose his own soul. (Mark 8:36). It is important to know that we don't stay connected trying to have the best of both worlds. Grandma said you can't have your 🪙 and eat it too. The Bible says no one can serve 2 masters he will love the one and hate the other he will hold to the one and despise the other. You cannot serve both God and mammon (money). Money comes with staying connected so it's not money 💵 itself it's the love of 💵 that is the root of all evil. (1 Timothy 6:10). Truly if we stay connected to the true vine we will be just fine. (John 15:1)

HE SAW ME TO DRAW ME

The Lord desires to draw all of mankind to him. Jesus said those that you gave me I have kept and none of them is lost. (John 17:12). He didn't come to do any of us in. God sent his son into the world not to condemn the world but that the world through him might be saved. (John 3:17). How did he see me Pastor? Answer: He is omnipresent (ever present everywhere). The eyes 👀of the Lord are in every place beholding (looking) at the evil and the good. (Proverbs 15:3). He sees us because he wants us to draw us. He will (desire) that all mankind be saved and come to the knowledge of the truth. (1 Timothy 2:4). The truth is God so loved the world that he gave his only begotten son that whosoever believe on him should not perish (spiritually die) but have everlasting life. (John 3:16). What does he do to draw us Pastor? Answer: He has already done it. With loving kindness have I drawn you (Jeremiah 31:3). What can I do Pastor to experience his love and Power? Answer: Receive the Holy Ghost. After the Holy Ghost comes upon you shall receive power and be witnesses unto me. (Acts 1:8). How can I get closer Pastor now that he has saw me? Answer: Draw near to God and he will draw near to you. (James 4:8)

LIFE WOULD BE MIGHTY GRIM IF IT WAS NOT FOR MIGHTY HIM

Life is challenging as it is. We have few days and full of trouble (Job 14:1). So life would be mighty grim if it was not for mighty him (Jesus). Truly if it had not been the Lord who was on our side we would have been swallowed up. (Psalms 124:1). It's not because of our goodness that we are here. It is of the Lord's mercies that we are not consumed, because his compassion fail us not. (Lamentations 3:22) I am certain that life would be mighty grim if it wasn't for mighty him. Jesus told his disciples that without me you can do nothing. (John 15:5). Life would be mighty grim had Jesus not been buried and rose again the 3rd day according to the scriptures. (1 Corinthians 15:4). If Jesus was not rained our faith would be in vain and we all would yet be in our sins. (Corinthians 15:17. Thank God for mighty him for without him life would be mighty grim.

LET US BRACE OURSELVES FOR WE ARE LIVING IN UNORDINARY TIMES

Let's brace ourselves (let's spiritually, mentally and physically prepare ourselves). My Pastor the late Bishop Edward L. Thomas would often say that these are the days that try Men souls. These days are of few days and full of trouble. (Job 14:1). We should brace ourselves for all that Jesus said is going to come to pass. You will hear 🎵of wars and rumors of wars. (Matthew 24:6). Let's brace ourselves for what Paul said. In the last days perilous(Dangerous) times will come. Mankind will become lovers of pleasure more than lovers of God. (2 Timothy 3:4) These are indeed unordinary times. John said there is coming a time when they will kill you and 🙂think they doing God service (ISIS, Domestic terrorist, etc....) (John 16:2). Therefore it is vital that we whoever has 🎵let them 🎵what the spirit says to the church. (Revelation 2:29). I 🎵the spirit saying it's high time (about time) that we wake out of sleep 😊. For our salvation (deliverance) is nearer than when we first believed (Romans 13:11). Lets help one another to prepare and get through these unordinary times. Be encouraged to know that if God be for us who can be against us. (Romans 8:31)

LET US BRACE OURSELVES FOR WE ARE LIVING IN UNORDINARY TIMES PART 2

We are living in unordinary times PART 2-The unordinary times get the more we should brace ourselves.5 points of signs of unordinary times.

POINT 1- People loved darkness rather than the light because their deeds were evil. (John 3:19).

Point2- Because iniquity shall abound the love of many shall wax cold (Matthew 24:12).

POINT 3- In the latter times some shall depart from the faith giving heed to seducing spirits and doctrines (teachings) of devils. (1 Timothy 4:1).

POINT 4- People will not endure (put up with) sound doctrine (teaching). But after their own lust (desires) shall heap to themselves teachers having itching ears. Turning away from the truth and turning to fables. (2 Timothy 4:3).

POINT 5-There will be false Prophets that come to you in sheep 🐑 clothing but on the inside they are ravening wolves 🐺. (Matthew 7:15). I could not help others if I didn't give out the things to be aware of in order for you to brace yourself. There are imitators that would deceive the very elect if it was possible. (Matthew 24:24). To no surprise the devil has transformed himself to an angel of light. (2 Corinthians 11:14). So let's brace ourselves satan gets in people. They may look the part but I heard the time was coming when people will have a form of Godliness but deny the power there of. He said we are to turn away from them. (2 Timothy 3:5). Pastor how will we know so we can brace ourselves? You will know them by their fruit. A corrupt tree can't bring forth good fruit. A good tree can not bring forth corrupt fruit. (Matthew 7:20).

Don't Look At The Problem Look At The Promise Part 2

Look at the Promise part 2: We now look at the promises of God. First of all when he makes a promise I come to know as Barretta said: You can take it to the bank. His foundation stand sure. (2nd Timothy 2:19). For his promises are yes and amen. (2 Corinthians 1:20). 5 points of Promise over our problems.

POINT 1- Problem Trouble (Job 14:1)

Promise: God is our refuge and strength a very present help in trouble (Psalms 46:1)

POINT 2-Problem Affliction (1st Peter 5:9)

Promise- God deliver us out of them all. (Psalms 34:19).

POINT 3- Problem- Persecution (2nd Timothy 3:12)

Promise- We are persecuted but not forsaken. (2nd Corinthians 4:9).

Point 4-Problem Enemies Psalms 27:2)

Promise- When the enemy shall come in like a flood. The spirit of the Lord will lift up a standard. (Isaiah 59:19).

Point 5- Problem- the devil (1st Peter 5:8)

Promise- Resist the devil and he will flee from you. (James 4:7).

When We Are Unified, Satan Is Terrified & God Is Glorified

I am led to talk on unity tonight as part 2 of this message. Many as be led of the spirit they are the sons/daughters of God. (Romans 8:14). Throughout biblical times unity in God always bring blessings and great results. 5 points where unity prevailed.

POINT 1- In the fiery furnace 3 were thrown in. Counselor did not we put in 3? I see 4 men walking around loose and the 4ᵗʰ one looks like the form of the son of God. (Daniel 3:25).

POINT 2-4 leprous men. Why sit here till we die? They in unity moved and they prevailed. (2 Kings 7:3).

POINT 3- Gideons Army. God told him to go from 22,000 and use the 300 that lapped water like a dog 🐕. In unity 300 prevailed over the Midianites. (Judges 7:1-10).

POINT 4- Paul and Silas beaten and thrown in jail/ prison. In unity they prayed and praised God. At midnight 🕐God shook the foundation. (Acts 16:24-27)

POINT 5- When the day of Pentecost was fully come 120 was in the upper room in one place on one 1 accord (Unity) Suddenly there came a sound from heaven as a rushing and mighty wind 💨it filled all the house where they were sitting and they all were filled with the Holy Ghost and began to speak with other tongues as the spirit gave them utterance. ((Acts 2:1-38)

GET READY, GET SET, GROW!

Get ready! Get set!, GROW- This sermon title reminds us of when kids or track runners get ready for a race 🏃. The Christian journey is also described as a race. The race is not solely based on speed nor strength. The race is not given to the swift nor to the strong 💪(Ecclesiastes 9:11). The one that endure to the end will be saved. (Matthew 24:13). In order to win the race one must first get ready, by being born again. Jesus told Nicodemus you must be born again. (John 3:3, John 3:7). You get set by having faith. How is faith obtained? Faith comes by hearing and hearing by the word of God. (Romans 10:17). You may start out like a 👶baby that desire the sincere milk 🍼of the word that you may grow thereby. (1 Peter 2:2). You grow in grace and in the knowledge of the Lord Jesus Christ. (2 Peter 3:18). Growing is a mindset of a child, teenager. We should have that mindset to grow spiritually. Jesus was praying and laying hands on children and those that had not grown didn't understand. He proceeded to take a child in his arms and said to them. Except you humble yourself as this child 👧 you shall in no wise enter the kingdom of God. (Luke 18:17).

Let's Not Focus On Our Been Through, Let's Focus On Our Breakthrough

From the 📖study of God word and from experience I find that we should put our focus 👀on our breakthrough far more than our been through. Our been through may overwhelm us. David said when my heart overwhelm me lead me to the rock that is higher than I (Psalms 61:2). David focus was on his breakthrough. In spite of the need for help he focused on his breakthrough. He said I will lift my 👀to the hills from where my help comes my help comes from the Lord who made the heaven and earth. (Psalms 121:1). Regardless of the enemy he focused on the breakthrough. He said the Lord is my light and my salvation whom shall I fear? The Lord is the strength of my life whom shall I be afraid? (Psalms 27:1). We are encouraged throughout the scriptures to focus on the God that is able to do exceedingly abundantly above all that we ask or think 😊 according to the power that work in us. (Ephesians 3:20). Focusing on the breakthrough will help us to be confident of this very thing that he which has begun a good work in you will perform (complete) it until the day of Jesus Christ (Philippians 1:6). Focusing on the breakthrough will aid us to not be weary in well doing for in due season we will reap if we faint not. (Galatians 6:9). May we ever focus on the breakthrough by looking to Jesus the author and finisher of our faith. (Hebrews 12:2).

GOD GAVE THE BEST, LET'S GIVE HIM OUR YES PART 2

PART2- As Marie Brock said God always give his best and has nothing but the best for us. I use to hear my Aunt Ernestine Montgomery say who wouldn't serve a God like him? Yet we have those that say there is no God. A fool has said in his heart that there is no God. (Psalms 14:1). He is the best in the fact that he loves us unconditionally (Agape Love) But God commend his love toward us in that while we were yet sinners, Christ died for us. (Romans 5:8). His peace is the best. Peace I leave with you, my peace I give to you, not as the world give, give I unto you. (John 14:27). When it comes to making promises he is the best. God is not slack (Slow) concerning his promise as some men count slackness but he is long suffering toward us not willing that any should perish but that all should come to repentance. (2 Peter 3:9). The list goes on and on about revealing through the scriptures that we have the best available. Eye 👁 has not seen 👁 has not heard neither has it entered into the heart ♥ of mankind what God has prepared for them that love him. (1 Corinthians 2:9). Part 3 we shall discuss to what is our response to having the very best available to us? Country Wayne says let that sizzle in your spirit.

GOD GAVE THE BEST, LET'S GIVE HIM OUR YES PART 3

PART 3- Jesus is the best that there is or ever will be. There is none beside me . I am the Lord and there is none else. (Isaiah 45:6). There is none like me (Isaiah 46:9). Him being the best should get a proper response from all of us. 5 Points of response

POINT 1- His goodness- our response it lead us to repentance. (Romans 2:4).

POINT 2- His Love- our response. We love him because he first loved us. (1 John 4:19).

POINT 3-For rest- Our response. Come to me all that labor and are heavy laden and I will give you rest. (Matthew 11:28).

POINT 4-For Peace- our response keep our minds on him. I will keep them in perfect peace whose mind is stayed on thee. (Isaiah 26:3).

For the gift of the Holy Ghost. Our response. Repent and be baptized every one of you in the name (Authority, Character) Lord Jesus Christ for the remission (Removal) of your sins and you shall receive the gift of the Holy Ghost. (Acts 2:38). That's point 5. Be blessed again I am honored that you view these messages. And read the context of messages. You are an inspiration to me. You can watch these messages at any time by going to YouTube and type in the WORD MINISTRIES WITH PASTOR BILLY BEDFORD.

STRIVE TO STAY ALIVE
WITH NO TIME FOR JIVE

In these times of few days and full of trouble (Job 14:1). We find ourselves striving to stay alive. In the midst of a pandemic. Keep striving to stay alive even if you have to tell yourself. Self I shall not die but live and declare the works of the Lord. (Psalms 118:17). Perhaps you feel you don't have much faith to make it. I say to you, you don't have to have a whole LOT, just use the little you GOT. If you have faith as a grain of a mustard seed. You can speak to mountains and tell them to be moved. If you doubt not in your heart but believe those things you say shall come to pass you shall have whatever you say. (Mark 11:22-24). The woman with the issue of blood for 12 years kept striving. If I may but touch the hem of his garment I shall be made whole. (Matthew 9:20). Blind Bartemaeus kept on striving. When he heard Jesus was passing by he cried out loudly Jesus thou son of David have mercy on me. There will be times it doesn't look like you can take anymore. I say to you be not weary in well doing for in due season you will reap if you faint not. (Galatians 6:9). Live your life with this principle. He that has begun a good work in you will perform (complete)it until the day of Jesus Christ (Philippians 1:6). Keep striving for Jesus said I am come that you might have life and have it more abundantly (John 10:10)

STRIVE TO STAY ALIVE WITH NO TIME FOR JIVE PART 2

Part2-When one is striving to stay alive the one thing they don't have time for is JIVE (Foolish, deceptive, unserious). When we were in the world we went along with the song: Everybody plays the fool sometimes, no exception to the rule. That was in our B C days (Before Christ) came in our lives. We now have no time for jive. If anyone be in Christ they are a new creation, old things are passed away and behold all things become new. (2 Corinthians 5:17). We use to be about our 🐀killing. We now must be about our father's business. (Luke 2:49). Love them and leave them that is what you used to do. Use and abuse them may have been your claim to fame. I am glad the Lord didn't jive with us. He said I will never leave you or forsake you. (Hebrews 13:5). While we were in our sin and in our gin 🍷(I know some of y'all saying that's not the color of gin it's spiked with koolaid. 😄I was a bit humorous tonight because I know someone reading this need to remember from where God has brought you from. I close with encouragement to you be confident of this very thing that he which has begun a good work in you will perform it (Complete) until the day of Jesus Christ. (Philippians 1:6). Laughter is good for you. It's like medicine. (Psalms 126:2) (Ecclesiastes 3:4) (Proverbs 17:22).

DON'T FEAR DON'T DREAD, GOD IS THE LIFTER OF OUR HEAD

In spite of all that is going on within us and around us. God does not want us to fear. God has not given us a spirit of fear but of power, love, and a sound mind. (2nd Timothy 1:7). God does not want us to dread (Be afraid) You will have some enemies but don't you fear. David said the Lord is my light and my salvation whom shall I fear. The Lord is the strength of my life of whom shall I be afraid? (Psalms 27:1). You will face intimidators but don't dread. God told Jeremiah to be not afraid of their faces. (Jeremiah 1:8). David also said the Lord is on my side I will not fear. What can man do to me? (Psalms 118:6). The one we should fear is the Lord. The fear of the Lord is the beginning of wisdom. (Proverbs 9:10). The devil has told you he was going to kill you. That's what he comes for. To steal, to KILL and to destroy. (John 10:10). Don't fear the one that can only kill the body. Fear the one (Jesus) that can kill the body and soul in hell. (Matthew 10:28).

DON'T FEAR DON'T DREAD, GOD IS THE LIFTER OF OUR HEAD PART 2

Don't fear don't dread PART 2-Do not fear is written in the Bible 365 times (equal to every day of the year). It's not that we don't have some scary things in our life. It's because God will never leave us or forsake us. (Hebrews 13:5) He said I will be with you always even to the end of the world. (Matthew 28:20).When facing a harrowing situation you have to look higher than Doctor 🗄, Lawyer, Indian chief, higher than yourself. David said when my heart overwhelms me, lead me to the rock that is higher than I. (Psalms 61:2). You are in need of help, I encourage you to lift your eyes 👀to the hills from where comes your help, your help comes from the Lord which made the heaven and earth. (Psalms 121:1). If you need help right now, fast, quick, and in a hurry don't fear. God is our refuge and strength a very present help in trouble. (Psalms 46:1). God said be anxious for nothing and pray about everything. (Philippians 4:6) Paraphrasing. How can we not fear. By casting all your care upon him for he cares for you. (1 Peter 5:7). In closing let us rely on the words of David when facing danger and possibly death. He said Lord you a shield 🛡for me my Glory and the lifter of my head. (Psalms 3:3)

Jesus First Of All And In All Is Our Call

There is a figure of speech that says don't put the cart before the horse 🐴. That means first things first. The one that should be first in all our lives is the Lord. To my Spanish students he should be numero uno. He desires/ require to be number 1. Remember what you told that young lady/ man? If I can't be number 1, I won't be number 2. God is the same for he is a jealous God. (Deuteronomy 4:24). Even his name is Jealous. (Exodus 34:14). You may say I need things. God knows we have need of things (Luke 12:30). He just wants us to have him first. Seek you first the kingdom of God (His way of doing things) and his righteousness and all these things will be added to you. (Matthew 6:33). When we allow him to have preeminence (Surpassing all others) (Colossians 1:18). We will prosper and be in health even as our soul shall prosper (3 John 1:2) Stay tunes for PART 2- Jesus First of All and in all.

JESUS FIRST OF ALL AND IN ALL IS OUR CALL PART 2

Jesus first of all PART 2- Even thou the Lord desire to be first in our life. He doesn't force himself upon any of us. Whosoever will let them take of the water of life freely (Revelations 22:17). 5 points as to why it's important we allow him to be first and foremost.

POINT 1-He said we shall have no other gods before him. (Exodus 20:3).

POINT 2-Without him we can do nothing. (John 15:5).

POINT 3- With him there is life. Without him we don't have life They that have the son has life. They that don't have the son (Jesus) doesn't have life (Spiritual life) (1 John 5:12).

POINT 4-When he is first . You have power. After the Holy Ghost comes upon you will have power. (Acts 1:8)

POINT 5-When he is first and you are filled with the Holy Ghost you will have love in your heart. The love of God is shed abroad in our hearts by the Holy Ghost (Romans 5:5)

Short Term PAIN For A Long Term GAIN

From studying 📖 and from experience I come to know that In this life we will have some pain. Man that is born of a woman is of few days and full of trouble. (Job14:1). I am thankful that pain is short term. The anger of the Lord is but a moment, weeping may endure for a night but joy comes in the morning. (Psalms 30:5). We can be encouraged to know that short term pain is going to lead to long term gain. If we suffer with him (Short term) we shall also reign with him (Long term.) (2 Timothy 2:12). I reckon that the sufferings of this present time (Short term) are not worthy to be compared to the Glory that's going to be revealed in us (Long term). After you have suffered a while (Short term) then I will make you perfect (Complete) Establish, strengthen, settle you (Long term) (1 Peter 5:10). Let us not be weary in well doing (Short term) For you shall reap in due season if we faint not (Long term). (Galatians 6:9). If you suffer for righteousness sake (Short term) Happy are you (Long term) (1 Peter 3:14).

Short Term PAIN For A Long Term GAIN Part 2

Short term PAIN for long term GAIN PART 2- Be encouraged to know that in all that you been through/ going through that it's short term/ temporary and is going to benefit you long TERM Not some things but ALL things work together to the good of them that love God and are the called according to his purpose. (Romans 8:28). Your 😄 are short term. The anger of the Lord is but a moment, weeping may endure for a night but Joy comes in the morning (Psalms 30:5). You that are facing some health issues or have love ones with health issues. I stop by YouTube/Facebook to tell somebody. That he was wounded for our transgressions bruised for our iniquities, the chastisement of our peace was upon him and by his stripes you are healed. (Isaiah 53:5). I prophecy to you tonight that has been waiting for a change a long time you are going to do like Job did. He said If a man die shall he live again, all the day and my appointed time will I wait upon my change (Job14:14).

TO GET HOME, YOU GOT TO GO BY ME

You have got to go by me PART 1- These are not my words to you but the words of Jesus to us all. We need to always hear what he says. They that have ears let them hear what the spirit says to the church (Revelations 2:29). In order to go to the eternal home with God the father we must go by Jesus. He said I am the door (Access way) of the sheep and by me if anyone enters they shall be saved. (John10:7). Pastor are you sure there is not another way besides going by Jesus? Jesus said all that climb up another way are thieves and robbers and don't/won't get in. (John 10:1). He told Thomas: I am the way the truth and the life. NO ONE comes to the father but by me. (John 14:6). Paul said neither is there salvation in any other. For there is no other name under heaven given among mankind whereby we MUST BE SAVED. (Acts 4:12). We don't make it home unless by Jesus For without me says Jesus you can do nothing. (John 15:5.) We can't pay our way home What shall it profit a man to gain the whole world and lose his own soul? What shall he give in exchange for his soul? Mark8:36-3

To Get Home, You Got To Go By Me Part 3

You got to go by me PART 3-Since none of us can come to the father but by him (John 14:6) We should desire to know what he says about REPENTANCE, just like we desire the windows of heaven open (Malachi 3:10). Repentance is to become Godly sorrow. Paul told the Corinthian church that he rejoiced not that they were made sorry but that they were made sorry after a Godly manner. For Godly sorrow work repentance to salvation. (1 Corinthians 7:9-10). Jesus hold repentance in high regard. He said Joy shall be in heaven over ONE SINNER that repent more than 99 just persons that need no repentance. (Luke 15:7). John the Baptist said REPENT for the Kingdom of heaven is at hand. (Matthew 3:2) Luke said except you REPENT you shall all likewise perish (Luke 13:3). Paul said God in Times past winked at our sins. But now he is commanding mankind everywhere to REPENT (Acts 17:30). When the house of Israel was pricked in their heart they said men and brethren what must we do? Peter said REPENT every one of you and be baptized in the name (Authority, Character) Lord Jesus Christ for the remission of your sins and you shall receive the gift of the Holy Ghost (Acts 2:38).

JESUS DID NOT COME TO TAKE SIDES, HE CAME TO TAKE OVER

He came to take over PART 2- Jesus came to take over not in an Authoritarian (enforcing authority) way. He came to take over in a Powerful way. He declared All power is given to me in heaven and in earth. (Matthew 28:18)

Point 2- He came to take over in fulfillment of Prophecy (The Government shall be laid upon his shoulder. (Isaiah 9:6)

Point 3-He came to take over to order our steps. The steps of a good man/woman are ordered by the Lord. (Psalms 37:23).

Point 4-He came to take over because we are like sheep and would not find our way out of a wet paper bag without him. All we are like sheep which as gone astray and turned everyone to their own way. (Isaiah 53:6).

POINT 5- He came to take over so that we could have eternal life. For the wages of sin is death but death but the gift of God is eternal life. (Romans 6:23).

WHEN YOU GIVE GOD THE KEY TO YOUR HEART, DON'T LET SATAN HAVE A SPARE

God desires to be the 🔑 to all our hearts. When he is the key we can/will love God with all our hearts, mind and soul. We will love our neighbor as ourselves. (Matthew 22:38-39).What about my past ? When you give God the 🔑. There is therefore NOW no condemnation to them which are in Christ Jesus who walk not after the flesh but after the spirit. (Romans 8:1)When he gets your heart you are no longer the same. If anyone be in Christ they are a new creation. Old things are passed away and behold all things are become new. (2 Corinthians 5:17) When you give God the 🔑 you are under new management. You are not your own for you are bought with a price. (1 Corinthians 6:19-20). In part 2 we shall cover the importance of not letting the devil have a spare. Be encouraged and blessed every one feel free to share and subscribe to this YouTube / Television ministry free of charge. By the way when we give God the 🔑 he receive us free of charge. Come without money come without price. (Isaiah 55:1).

When You Give GOD The Key To Your Heart, Don't Let Satan Have A Spare Part 3

Don't let satan have a spare 🔑PART 3-In order to not let satan have a spare 🔑, We should be FULLY persuaded that nothing shall be able to separate us from the love of God. (Romans 8:39). Often the biggest enemy to giving up the spare 🔑is the one in the mirror (Me, myself, and I) which is why we must deny ourselves take up our cross and follow him. (Matthew 16:24). We have a choice we can let God be the 🔑, or we can give satan a spare. God said I have set before you this day life and evil, death and good. (Deuteronomy 30:15). He said to choose life that you and your seed may live. (Deuteronomy 30:19). On mount Carmel there was a battle. They said if Lord be God then follow him. If baal (false god) be God then follow him. I thank God if we give God the 🔑he will answer by 🔥. (1 Kings 18:24). Let's not give satan a spare 🔑. For no one can serve two masters, they will love the one and hate the other they will hold to the one and despise the other. (Matthew 6:24).Lets be like Joshua and declare as for me and my house we will serve the Lord (Joshua 24:15).

THE LORD IS GOING TO STRAIGHTEN ALL OF THIS OUT

The virus ☀️ is one of the many things that the Lord is going to straighten out. To straighten means to fix or make right. God promise to make crooked places straight, elevate valleys (low places in our life). (Isaiah 40:4). Things that are going wrong he will make it right. He will set at liberty then that are bruised. Recovery of sight to the blind (including spiritual blind), to heal the broken-hearted. (Luke 4:18). God will strengthen out your brokenness. He heals the broken-hearted and he binds up their wounds. (Psalms 147:3) .I remember when I was sick and tired of being sick and tired. I stop by to tell someone that the Lord will straighten it out. Yes my sister he will receive you. Whoever come to me I in no wise (case) will cast them out. (John 6:37). Be encouraged brother the Lord will straighten it out for you. If anyone be in Christ they are a new creation, old things are passed away and behold all things become new. (2 Corinthians 5:17). If you don't know what to do. Do what David did. Lift your eyes to the hills from where your help comes. (Psalms 121:1). I prophesy to you that is reading this while experiencing anxiety. To cast all your cares upon him for he cares for you. (1 Peter 5:7).

LET'S TAKE OUR FAITH OUT OF MAN AND PLACE IT IN THE SAVIOR'S HANDS

It is the desire and the will of God that we put our faith in him. When they reminded Jesus of the fig tree he had cursed had dried up at the root. He told them to have faith in God. (Mark11:22). Taking your faith out of man includes yourself. Lean not to your own understanding but trust in the Lord in all your ways acknowledge him and he will direct your path. (Proverbs 3:5). Taking faith out of man means taking faith out of man made things. Things are going to perish (tear up, come to a close) with the using thereof. (Colossians 2:22). Taking faith out of man means taking your hope out of just this life alone. If in this life we only have hope we are of all mankind most miserable. (1 Corinthians 15:19) My hope (faith) is built on nothing less than Jesus blood and his righteousness. I dare not trust in the sweetest frame, but wholly lean on Jesus name. On Christ the solid rock I stand. All other grounds are sinking sand.

In the Midst of the Pandemic, Give HIM Praise Part 2

Praise him in the midst PART2: As we are in the midst of the corona virus It's important that we give God the praise in the midst. In the midst of all David was going through he declared that I will bless the Lord at all times and his praise shall continually be in my mouth. (Psalms 34:1). It is in our DNA to praise him. For praise is comely (becoming of us) for the upright. (Psalms 33:1). When Habakkuk was in lack he praised God in the Midst. No fruit on vine, no herd in the stalls, fields yield no meat , Yet will rejoice in the Lord. (Habakkuk 3:17). Paul and Silas had been beaten and thrown in jail. But they gave God the praise and at midnight he shook the foundation. They marched around the Jericho walls and on the 7th day they gave out a shout and the wall fell down. (Joshua 6:5-6). Be encouraged every one to praise him in the midst. What do you have to praise him for? His excellent greatness, His mighty acts. If you are reading this I want you to BREATHE in.... Now BREATHE out. That qualifies you to praise him. Let everything (everyone) that has BREATH PRAISE THE LORD!!! (Psalms 150:1-6).

YOU CAN STAY IF YOU DO IT GOD'S WAY PART 2

Do it God's way PART 2- One of the amazing things about God is that he still love us even when we don't do it his way. God commendeth his love toward us while we were yet sinners. (Romans 5:8). Don't fool yourself there are consequences to us doing it our way. Be not deceived God is not mocked whatsoever you sow that you shall also reap. (Galatians 6:7). God still love us thou he may have to whip us. Whom he loves he chasten. (Hebrews 12:8). If you want to stay in peace do it God way. He will keep them in perfect peace whose mind is stayed on him. (Isaiah 26/3). If you want to stay with the Gospel do it God way. They that take hold of the Gospel plough and look back is not fit (ready) for the kingdom of God (Luke 9:62) If you need help do it God way. David said I will lift my eyes to the hills from where my help comes. (Psalms 121:1)

THERE HAS TO BE A SHAKING IN ORDER FOR THERE TO BE A MAKING

I come to know that God allows some shaking (Trials, tribulations). I also come to know that it's for our making. In the world you will have tribulations but be of good cheer for I have overcome the world. (John 16:33). What am I to do when shaking with temptation? Count it all Joy when you fall into divers(different)temptations. (James 1:2) With every temptation God will make a way of escape so that you are able to make it. (1 Corinthians 10:13). We all must understand that to have a making there has to be a shaking. In all your getting get understanding (Proverbs 4:7). It's in the shaking that you find the joy of the Lord is your strength. (Nehemiah 8:10)

BE SAVED, BE HEALED, BE DELIVERED, & BE SET FREE

These are 4 things that the Lord desire all mankind to be. (SAVED, HEALED, DELIVERED, and set FREE). Let's begin with SAVED.

Jesus Christ came into this world to save sinners (1 Timothy 1:15)

It is his will that all mankind be saved. (1 Timothy 2:4)

The angel told Joseph that she (Mary) shall bring forth a son and that they would call his name Jesus, and he shall save his people from their sin. (Matthew 1:21)

If you are not saved I stopped by Facebook to tell somebody Jesus is looking for you 👀.(The son of mankind (Jesus) is come to seek 👀and to save whoever is lost.

(Luke 19:10).

You can and will be saved if you believe on him as the scripture have said for out of your belly (innermost) will flow rivers of living water. He was referring to his spirit because the Holy Ghost was not yet given. (John 7:38)

WHAT'S THE MATTER
WITH YOU? PART 2

What's the matter with you PART 2- This message is about Hannah who had something the matter with her for one she could not bear children (Because the Lord had shut up her womb.) To top it off her adversary (Peninnah was provoking her sore. (1 Samuel 1:1-10.) Perhaps you feel you have been held back from something you have wanted all your life and it has caused something to matter with you? I say to you that God has given us everything that pertain to life and Godliness. (2 Peter 1:3). The lord is always mindful of us. (Psalms 115:12). When something is the matter. The Heavenly Father know that you have need of things. (Matthew 6:32). It is the father's good pleasure to give you the Kingdom (Luke 12:32). So when something is the matter be not dismayed, whatever betides (Happens to you) God will take care of you. The songwriter said that God specializes in things that seem impossible. For with God all things are possible. (Matthew 19:26). Stay tuned tomorrow for part 3 because someone reading 📖right now has something the matter with them not just because of things but because of PEOPLE. We will cover that because Hannah had a person causing soreness upon her.

WHAT'S THE MATTER
WITH YOU? PART 3

What's the matter with you PART 3- Today we are going to focus on what to do when it's actually people that is causing something to be the matter with you. I give 5 points for Hannah had an adversary provoking her sore while she was going through.

POINT 1 - That person may be doing evil toward you. POINT 1- Fret not yourself because of evil doers nor be envious of workers of iniquity for they shall soon be cut down like the grass and wither as the green herb ❧ .(Psalms 37:1-2).

POINT 2- You been done wrong and it not sitting well with you. Do not be overcome with evil but overcome evil with good. (Romans 12:21)

POINT 3-You still are thinking of getting even with them. Recompense (pay) no one evil for evil. Vengeance is mine says God I will repay. (Romans 12:19).

POINT 4-What about my enemies? Love your enemies. (Luke 6:27)

POINT 5-You are tired of your kindness being taken for weakness. Let us not be weary in well doing for in due season we will reap if we faint not. (Galatians 6:9).

I AM COMING OUT
WITH MY HANDS UP

I am coming out with my hands up PART2-When we say that we are coming out with our hands up in essence we are saying we are coming out victorious. God causes us to always triumph in Christ. (2 Corinthians 2:14). Paul said that we are killed all the day long and are accounted as sheep for the slaughter, but we are more than a conqueror through him that love us. (Romans 8:36-37). You may be saying I want to come out with my hands up but I don't have a lot of faith. I say to you that you don't have to have a whole LOT just use the little you GOT. If you have faith as a grain of mustard seed you can speak to mountains and tell them to be removed. Doubt not in your heart but believe those things which you say shall come to pass you can have whatever you say. (Mark 11:22-24). You are coming out with your hands up not because of you but because God grace is sufficient for you in the time of your weakness his strength will be made perfect. (2 Corinthians 12:9). When you feel as though you can't. Say these words. I can do all things through Christ which strengthens me. (Philippians 4:13).

BE CAREFUL SNAKES ARE CRAWLING PART 2

Snakes are crawling PART 2- In part 1 we see that satan himself is the Snake. He is known in the Bible as a serpent that's more subtle (Crafty) than any beast of the field. (Genesis 3:1). He is also called that old serpent. (Revelations 20:2). God want us to be aware because that old serpent walks about as a roaring lion seeking who he can devour. (1 Peter 5:8). He has many tricks but Paul said that we are not ignorant of satan's devices. (2 Corinthians 2:11). I am going to have to do a part 3 for there is much to cover as to how the snake does his evil and we are sometimes not aware. I leave you with this Jesus sat at the table and said I have chosen 12 of you. And one of you (Judas) is a devil. (John 6:70). They began to say to him Lord is it I? (Matthew 26:20-26). So let us examine ourselves as to whether we be in the faith. (2 Corinthians 13:5). I know no one reading this wants to intentionally play the role of the snake . The best way to assure ourselves is to follow the first 2 Commandments. Love the Lord thy God with all your heart, mind with all your soul and with all your strength. The second is alike it. Love your neighbor as yourself. (Matthew 22:39-40).

BE CAREFUL SNAKES ARE CRAWLING PART 3

Snakes are crawling PART 3- In part 1 and 2 we taught that satan, is the snake that is crawling. We now focus on the fact that he not just one dressed in a red cape with pointed horns and a long tail. That snake comes in the form of Beans. BEANS !! What kind of Beans? Answer: Human beings !! Yes if we let him he will crawl in people you thought as Pastor Lonnie Orr once said got angel wings. No wonder for satan has transformed himself to look like an angel of light. (2 Corinthians 11:14). The Bible says in the end time there are going to be false prophets will rise among us and shall deceive many (Matthew 24:11). Jesus told us to be aware of false prophets. They come to you in sheep clothing but inwardly they are ravening wolves .(Matthew 7:15). How will we know them snakes. Every tree will be known by its fruit. (Matthew 12:33). Snakes also come in the form false doctrines/ teachings. In the last days people will have itching ears and will not endure/ put up with sound doctrine. (2 Timothy 4:3). In the latter times some shall depart/ leave the faith giving heed to doctrines of devils and seducing spirits (1Timothy 4:1. Snakes are crawling so be careful for we know if he got false prophets and false teachers and false doctrines he will slither and crawl into any one that let him in. I hear James saying submit (Obey) yourselves to God resists the devil and he will flee from you (James 4:7)

I Can't Stop Now

I give encouragement to you that are going through trials and tests. That you can't stop now. You have come too far from where you started from. Let us not be weary in well doing for in due season we will reap if we faint not. (Galatians 6:9) 5 points to give you the determination that you can't stop now.

POINT 1- ENDURANCE- Endure hardness as a good soldier of Jesus Christ. (2 Timothy 2:3).

POINT 2- Faith- Without faith it is impossible to please God, they that come to him must believe that he is and that he is a rewarder of them that diligently seek him. (Hebrews 11:6)

POINT 3- CONFIDENCE- Being confident of this very thing that he which has begun a good work in you will perform it until the day of Jesus Christ. (Philippians 1:6)

POINT 4-Deny self- If anyone will be my disciple let him deny himself take up his cross and follow me. (Matthew 16:24)

POINT 5- Receive Power- After the Holy Ghost has come upon you shall receive power. (Acts 1:8)

I CAN'T STOP NOW PART 2

I can't stop now!! PART 2-The journey is tedious (Long, and tiresome) but I prophesy to you in particular as confirmation to your saying not long ago that I can't stop now. Things and people have had you to shed many a tear 😭lately, please know that weeping 😭May endure for a night but joy comes in the morning,

(Psalms 30:5). For they that sow in tears 😭shall reap in joy. (Psalms 126:5). But Pastor Billy you don't know how hectic my life is right now. That's true, but let me tell you what we both can know. And we know that all things work together to the good to them that Love God and are the called according to his purpose. (Romans 8:28). What is happening to you doesn't feel good. The devil is on your track trying to turn you back. You can't stop now what was meant for evil God is turning it around for your good. (Genesis 50:20). Don't stop keep pressing to the mark. (Philippians 3:14). Don't stop. Be steadfast, immovable always abounding in the work of the Lord for as much as you know that your labor is not in vain in the Lord (1 Corinthians 15:58).

YOU CAN STAND THE TEST WHEN YOU HAVE THE VERY BEST

We all in some form have faced some tests. Job said anyone that is born of a woman is of few days and full of trouble. (Job 14:1). Your test could be persecution. They that live Godly in Christ Jesus shall suffer persecution. (2 Timothy 3:12). Your test might be afflictions. Many are the afflictions of the righteous. (Psalms 34:19). Be encouraged to know that in spite of the trouble. God is a very present help in trouble. (Psalms 46:1). When you have the very best (Jesus) you can stand the test of persecution. We are persecuted but not forsaken. (2 Corinthians 4:9). He is there when you have affliction. In the latter portion of Psalms 19 it says But God delivers them out of them all. (Psalms 34:19). Be encouraged to know that you can stand the test for if God be for us who can be against us. (Romans 8:31). Help me out if you will by like, share, and subscribe to my YouTube channel by simply hit the subscribe button free of charge. Thanks and God bless you.

LET'S FOCUS ON THE SON, FOR HE WILL GET IT DONE

PART 2- Part 1 we noted the importance of focusing on Jesus with our eyes 👀fixated on him (PSALMS 121:1). Also our minds 😵focused on him. (Philippians 2:5). It is also important that our heart is focused. For with the heart mankind believes unto righteousness. (Romans 10:9) The heart should be focused because out of the heart are the issues of life. (Proverbs 4:23).what we put-allow in our heart we become that. (As one think 👅in their heart so they are. (Proverbs 23:7). Lastly our words from our mouth 👄must be done with focus. Death and life lies within the power of the tongue. (Proverbs 18:21). Paul said out of the same fountain (mouth) comes both sweet water 🐚and bitter we bless God with it and turn and curse with it. (James 3:9,10). Stay focused and we can with our mouth speak to mountains and tell them to be removed. If we doubt not in our heart but believe those things which we say we can have whatever we say. (Mark 11:22).

FROM A SINNER TO A WINNER

From a Sinner to a Winner part 4-In conclusion of this series we now focus on the Pharisee (member) of a party that believed in the resurrection and followed traditions not ascribed in the Bible) We should not want to be like them if we intend to inherit the Kingdom of God. Except your righteousness exceed (Go beyond) that of the scribes and Pharisees you shall in no case inherit the kingdom of God. (Matthew 5:20). 5 points as to why we must not be like this pharisee.

POINT 1- He came with pride. God resists the Proud. (1 Peter 5:5).

POINT 2- He was high minded- Think 😊not yourselves more highly than you ought to think. (Romans 12:3)

POINT 3- He was boasting of himself. You are saved by Grace through faith not of works, not of yourself lest any man should boast it is the gift of God. (Ephesians 2:8)

POINT 4-He prayed selfish. When you pray enter in your secret closet and God who see you secretly will reward you openly. (Matthew 6:6)

POINT 5-He had wrong motives towards giving, fasting, prayer, etc... All the ways of mankind are right (in their eyes) But God weighs the spirit (motives) (Proverbs 16:2)

FROM A SINNER TO A WINNER PART 2

From a Sinner to a Winner PART 2- Part 1 we talked about the tax collector that went to God as a Sinner as and came back a WINNER!! We now focus on what caused us to be a Sinner in the first place. I will say it wasn't all your fault or your parent's fault. Let's first hear from David. I was shaped in iniquity and in sin did my mother conceive me. (Psalms 51:5). So you mean we came here a Sinner? Yes! How so? By one man (Adam) sin entered into the world so death was passed upon all mankind for all have sinned. (Romans 12:5). By one man's disobedience (Adam) many (you and I) were made sinners. (Romans 11:19). How then can we become winners? Keep reading ⬜BOO BOO. By one man's obedience (Jesus) shall many be made/declared (Justified) righteous. (Romans 12:19). I know you have someone at your cousin church that may say they have not sinned All have sinned and come short of the glory of God. (Romans 3:23). Thankful that we all can come from a sinner to a winner if we ask him to have mercy (Luke 18:13). The wages of sin is death (can't win like that) But the gift of God is Eternal life (Romans 6:23) You are a winner like that From A Sinner To A Winner Part 3

FROM A SINNER TO A WINNER PART 3

From a Sinner to a Winner PART 3-In part 1 we covered the tax collector that became a winner by humbling himself (1 Peter 5:7). Part 2 we discussed when/ how we became a sinner when by one man (Adam) sin entered into the world (Romans 5:12). Part 3 I want to encourage each one that is a winner and those that desire to be a winner and may be struggling or losing on every hand. 5 points in context of being a winner.

POINT 1- Confidence. Being CONFIDENT of this very thing that he (Jesus) who has begun a work in you will perform/complete it until the day of Jesus Christ. (Philippians 1:6)

POINT 2- Don't faint. Let us not be weary in well doing for in due season we will reap if we faint not. (Galatians 6:9)

Point 3- He will cause you to be a winner. He causes us to always triumph. (2 Corinthians 2.14?

POINT 4-You can do it. I can do all things through Christ which strengthens me.(Philippians 4:13)

POINT 5-Know who you are and whose you are. We are more than a conqueror through him that love us.(Romans 8:37)

From a Sinner to a Winner PART 2- Part 1 we talked about the tax collector that went to God as a Sinner as and came back a WINNER!! We now focus on what caused us to be a Sinner in the first place. I will say it wasn't all your fault or your parents fault. Let's first hear from David. I was shaped in iniquity and in sin did my mother conceive me. (Psalms 51:5). So you mean we came here a Sinner? Yes! How so? By one man(Adam) sin entered into the world so death was passed upon all mankind for all have sinned.(Romans 12:5). By one man's disobedience(Adam) many(you and

I) were made sinners.(Romans 11:19). How then can we become winners? Keep reading 📖BOO BOO. By one man's obedience (Jesus) shall many be made/declared(Justified)righteous.(Romans 12:19). I know you have someone at your cousin's church that may say they have not sinned. All have sinned and come short of the glory of God.(Romans 3:23). Thankful that we all can come from a sinner to a winner if we ask him to have mercy (Luke 18:13). The wages of sin is death (can't win like that) But the gift of God is Eternal life(Romans 6:23) You are a winner like that

LEAN ON ME

There comes a time in all our lives that we someone to lean on. That someone is Jesus. Helen Miller said when your load get heavy Jesus said you can lean on me. He said come to me all that labor and are heavy laden and I will give you rest. (Matthew 11:28). We can always lean on Jesus. He said I will never leave you or forsake you. (Hebrews 13.5). As a matter of fact I will be with you always even to the end I. (Matthew 28:20). David said I was young but now am old, yet have never seen the righteous forsaken or his seed begging bread ▢. (Psalms 37:25). If your heart is broken you can lean on Jesus. He is near them with a broken heart and save those that have a contrite spirit. (Psalms 34:18). When anxiety and stress arise you can lean on Jesus. Casting all your care upon him for he cares for you. (1 Peter 5:7).

LEAN ON ME PART 2

LEAN ON ME PART TWO: From experience and study 📖 of the word. I can testify that we can lean on Jesus. Helen Miller said he won't let you fall. Now unto him who is able to keep you from falling. (Jude 1:24). I give 5 points that need to be in place in our lives in order to effectively lean on Jesus.

POINT 1- We must trust him, not ourselves. Lean not to your own understanding but trust in the Lord in all your ways acknowledge him and he will direct your path. (Proverbs 3:5).

POINT 2- we must have faith. For without faith it is impossible to please him. They that come to God must believe that he is and that he is a rewarder of them that diligently seek him. (Hebrews 11:6).

POINT 3- get self out of the way. If anyone will be his disciple let them deny themselves take up their cross and follow him. (MATTHEW 24:16).

POINT 4-Come to him Come unto me all that labor and are heavy laden and I will give you rest (Matthew 11:28.

POINT 5-Give yourself to him. I beseech therefore brethren by the mercies of God that you present your bodies as a living sacrifice holy and acceptable to God which is your reasonable service Be not conformed to this world but be transformed by the renewing of your mind that you may prove that which is good and acceptable the perfect will of God. (Romans 12:1)

HEAR THE WORD AND LIVE

We can eat healthy and it will significantly help us to live. We can exercise and take relatively good care of our bodies to help us live. In order to live the life God will have us to live we all need to hear 👂the word of God and we shall truly live. The word Bible) has the power/ instruction that will cause us to live. Revelation says they that have 👂let them hear 👂what the spirit says to the church. (Revelation 2:29). Hear the word and live for it is powerful and sharper than any two edged ⚔sword. (Hebrews 4:12). Hear the word and live the psalmist say it is a 🪔lamp to our feet 👣and a light 💡to our path (Psalms 119:105). Jeremiah say it like a hammer 🔨that break the rock in pieces. (Jeremiah 23:29). Hear the word and live Paul said the Gospel (Good news) is the power of God unto salvation. (Romans 1:16). In the context of this sermon Ezekiel Prophesied to the dry bones (The lost house of Israel) To hear the word and live.(Ezekiel 37:4)

Hear The Word
And Live Part 2

PART 2: The word of God is vital to our living. The word will make us free. You shall know the truth and the truth will make you free (John 8:32). The word is what sanctify (set apart) us. You are sanctified through the truth. Thy word is truth. (John 17:1). A good indication that the word is giving you life is that Jesus said everyone that is of the truth hears my voice. (John 18:37). Therefore we should receive with meekness (humble) the engrafted (Implanted). Actually rooted in your heart.). Which is able to save your soul. But be DOERS and not Hearers only deceiving your own selves. (James 1:20-22.)

Let's Not Focus On Our Setback Let's focus On Our Comeback

Paul said in the last days perilous (full of danger or risk) times shall come. (2 Timothy 3:1). Within these times we may face some setbacks. Maya Angelou said you may face some defeats but you must not be defeated. Therefore we must not focus on the setback we must focus on the comeback. In spite of the setback in due season we reap if we shall reap if we faint not. (Galatians 6:9). When the enemy comes in like a flood. Focus on the comeback for the spirit will lift up a standard against him. Isaiah 59:19). Much is on you and at you but focus on the comeback. For greater is he that is within you than he that is in the world. (1 John 4:4). It is challenging I agree but be encouraged to focus on the comeback. For no weapon formed against you will prosper. (Isaiah 54:17).

THE END RESULT OF
SAYING YES I CAN

The late mother Jeanette Cunningham (who lived to be 102 years old) was notable for telling all her students she taught and Sunday school and church affiliates, etc... If you told her you can't do something. She would firmly say YES YOU CAN !! YES YOU CAN!! Apostle Paul said I can do all things through Christ which strengthens me. (Philippians 4:13. Be encouraged to know that YES YOU CAN!! He is faithful (Jesus) that promised. (Hebrews 10:23). Yes you can not because you are so strong. But because his promises are yes and amen. (2 Corinthians 1:20). Yes you can because he always causes us to triumph. (2 Corinthians 2:14). Yes you can because if you abide (remain) in him and his word in you that you can ask what you will and it shall be done. (John 15:5). Yes you can because whatever you ask in his name that will he do. (John 14:13). Yes you can because you are more than a conqueror through him that love us. (Romans 8:37).

WHERE DO WE GO FROM HERE?

In life we can find ourselves asking this question (Where do we go from here?). We don't want to look back. Remember Lots wife. She looked back and turned to a pillar of 🜂. (Genesis 19:26). We don't want to become stagnated in the same place. Jesus said I must be about my father's work. (Luke 2:49). We don't want/need to be stuck in the past. Paul said forgetting those things which are behind and reaching forth to those things which are before me. I press toward the mark of the high calling of God which is in Christ Jesus. (Philippians 3:14). Where do we go from here? May we all be encouraged to be steadfast, unmovable, always abiding in the work of the Lord for as much as you know that your labor is not in vain in the Lord. (1 Corinthians 15:58).

WHERE DO WE GO FROM HERE? PART 2

Life's challenges will at times have us asking questions such as this. Perhaps you have looked to the left and to the right with seemingly nowhere to look for help out of a crucial situation. I encourage you to lift your eyes 👀to the hills from which come your help. Your help comes from the Lord who made the heaven and earth. (Psalms 121:1). When you have anxiety and life is stressful. We should be casting (throwing) all our cares (Anxieties) upon him for he cares for you. (1 Peter 5:7). In a time when many had left and followed Jesus no more. He turned to the 12 and asked will you also go away? They said where can we go? You have the words to eternal life. (John 6:66,67).

JUST LET BE WHO I AM

Moses asked God who should he tell them that sent me. God said tell them that I am sent you. (Exodus 3:14). He is yet and still the I Am. We only need to do is let (Allow) him to be I am. He is the I am deliverer. Stand still and see the salvation (deliverance)of the Lord. (Exodus 14:13). If you are hungry for better things in life. Let him be who I am. I am the Bread of life. (John 6:35). If you want to be with the father. Let me be who I am. I am the way the truth and the life. No one comes to the father but by me. (John 14:6).

HEAR THE WORD & LIVE PART 2

PART 2: The word of God is vital to our living. The word will make us free. You shall know the truth and the truth will make you free (John 8:32). The word is what sanctify (set apart) us. You are sanctified through the truth. Thy word is truth. (John 17:1). A good indication that the word is giving you life is that Jesus said everyone that is of the truth hears my voice. (John 18:37). Therefore we should receive with meekness (humble) the engrafted (Implanted). (Actually rooted in your heart). Which is able to save your soul. But be DOERS and not Hearers only deceiving your own selves. (James 1:20-22.)

GOD GIVES US FAR MORE THAN HE ASK OF US

As a child I didn't fully understand Big Momma, and Aunt Lula Mae, when they use to say: Who wouldn't serve a God like this. Like Paul when I was a child I thought ▬as a child, spoke as a child and did childish things. (1 Corinthians 13:11). I now know and fully understand for he is a God that gives far more to us than he asks of us. The return is great. Give what he asks and he will open the windows of heaven and pour you out a blessing not room enough for you to receive. (Malachi 3:10). Give and watch him give back far more. Give and it shall be given unto you.1. Good measure. 2.Pressed down. 3. Shaken together. 4. Running over. 5. Men/mankind shall give into your bosom. 6. What measure you mete. 7. It shall be meted back to you. (Luke 6:38). Bear in mind that he gives far more than material blessings. EXAMPLE: Everlasting life (John 3:16). Peace (John 14:27). Joy (Psalms 30:5).

FOR THE REAL POWER, GO TO THE POWER SOURCE

We as a whole tend to want what is real. Many like coca-cola (it's called the real thing). But when I need a Divine connection coca-cola can't help me. The real source for connection is Jesus. He said I am the true vine. (John 15:1). It is said that Campbell 🥫soup is mmmm good. Yet when I need a breakthrough, the taste of Campbell soup may not hit the spot. David said O taste and see that the Lord is good. (Psalms 34:8). When your spiritual lights from a storm ⚡. Alabama power can't restore you. You can go to the power source he will restore you. Jesus said I am the light of the world. (John 9:5). I ask that you share with others for we all need to go to him for he is the power source.

LET'S ALL MAKE THE SON OUR NUMBER ONE

There are enormous essential benefits to making the SON (Jesus Christ) number one in our lives. The songwriter said falling in Love with Jesus was the best thing I've ever done. 5 points of the many benefits of making/ choosing him to be number one in your life.

POINT 1-Everlasting life awaits you. God so loved the world that he gave his only begotten son. That whosoever believe in him should not perish but have everlasting life. (John 3:16).

POINT 2- He gives you power. After the Holy Ghost has come upon you, you shall have power to be witnesses unto me. (Acts 1:8).

POINT 3- He gives you safety/ protection. The name of the Lord is a strong tower, the righteous run into it and they are safe. (Proverbs 18:10).

POINT 4-He gives provision Seek first the Kingdom of God and his righteousness and all these things will be added to you.

POINT 5- He gives you the greatest love you will ever have Greater Love has no one than this than a man that will lay down his life for their friend (John 15:13).

YOU MAY BE BROKEN BUT
I CAN STILL USE YOU

In biblical times as well in everyday life there are those that have brokenness (belief and joy of who they are taken away). God can/will still use you in spite of your brokenness. 5 points as to what to do when feeling BROKEN.

POINT 1- Lean not to your own understanding but trust in the Lord with all your heart and in all your ways acknowledge him and he will direct your path. (Proverbs 3:5)

POINT 2-Be confident of this very thing that he which has begun a good work in you will perform (complete) until the day of Jesus Christ. (Philippians 1:6).

POINT 3- Let us not be weary in well doing for in due season we will reap if we faint not. (Galatians 6:9).

POINT 4- Lift your eyes to the hill from come your help. (Psalms 121:1)

POINT 5- Cast all your cares upon him for he cares for you. (1 Peter 5:7)

You May Be Broken But I Can Still Use You Part 2

To all that are BROKEN (OVERWHELMED BY GRIEF OR DISAPPOINTMENT) May you be encouraged to know that God can/will still use you. He comes to heal the broken-hearted. (Luke 4:18). For he heals the broken hearted and binds up their wounds (PSALMS 147:3). The psalmist said When my heart overwhelms me lead me to the rock that is higher than I. (Psalms 61:2). When our hearts are broken and our spirits are crushed that is when Jesus is right there. He is near them of a broken heart and saves/delivers them of a contrite spirit. (Psalms 34:18). God can use us in spite of our Brokenness

You May Be Broken But I Can Still Use You Part 3

Part 3: The context of this message is when Jeremiah went down to the Potters house and the Potter was molding the clay and when it was marred he made it again. Likewise the Lord is the POTTER and we are the CLAY. In order for the Lord to mend us we must give him the broken pieces ♥ . The clay (you and I) doesn't say to the POTTER (Jesus Christ) why have you made me like this (Romans 9:20). We are not our own, we are bought with a price. (1 Corinthians 7:23) . When we are broken we must not approach God Like burger 🍔King 👑and think 💭we will have it our way for our ways and our thoughts are not his ways and thoughts (Isaiah 55:8) He will use us in spite of our brokenness he will turn your mourning into dancing 💃(Psalms 30:11) He will give beauty for ashes, oil of joy for mourning and the garment of praise for the spirit of heaviness. (Isaiah 61:3).. If you are BROKEN, be encouraged for the POTTER (Jesus Christ) want to put you back together again.

IT WILL BE WORTH IT ALL

There is much going on in life right now both on the natural side of life and on the spiritual side of life. I can relate to both and can relate to wondering if it's worth it all. Well from experience and study ▭of the word of God. I rest assure you that it will be worth it all. Part 1 let's look at the natural side. There is injustice that we are still facing in 2020 (Amen somebody). Make you want to give someone a Mike Tyson uppercut ☒instead of turning the other cheek (Matthew 5:39). We may feel it's not worth it all and take matters into our own hands. Vengeance is mine says the Lord I will repay (Romans 12:19). You feel it's not worth it all and are ready to throw in the towel. Let us not be weary in well doing for in due season we will reap if we faint not. (Galatians 6:9).

I Can & I Will Prevail

As I post this video I am admittedly upset about the young man that lost his life at the hand/knee of a police 👮Monday in Minnesota 😣. Things such as this leaves one to wonder if they can or will prevail in life. I give 5 points as to how and why we can and will prevail.

POINT 1- We have to say it. Death and life are in the power of the tongue 👅(Proverbs 18:21).

You have to think 😳it. So a person think then so they are. (Proverbs 23:7)

POINT 3-Must have faith. Without faith it is impossible to please God, they that come to God must believe that he is and that he is a rewarder of them that diligently seek him. (Hebrews 11:6).

POINT 4-Know that Jesus will see to it that we prevail. He always causes us to always triumph. (2 Corinthians 2:14)

POINT 5 He is always there for us. If I be for you who can be against you (Romans 8:31)

I CAN & I WILL PREVAIL PART 2

PART 2: To PREVAIL is to prove more powerful than opposing forces. Having faith is essential for without faith it is impossible to please God. (Hebrews 11:5) Be encouraged to believe you are going to prevail in spite of what it looks like. We walk by faith and not by sight (2 Corinthians 5:7). If you think you are going to prevail you are well on your way. As one ● think in their heart so they are. (Proverbs 23:7) To prevail is to prove more powerful than opposing forces. In order to prove ourselves more powerful than opposing forces we must have faith. How do we get? Faith comes by hearing and hearing by the word of God (Romans 10:17 In spite of all going on within you and around you, you should tell yourself that you can and you will prevail. Power of life and death lies within the tongue ⋃(Proverbs 18:21)

LET'S WALK WITH INTENT & INTENSITY PART 2

In part 1 we gave 5 points of walking with intent (paying close attention to what you are doing). Part 2 we give 5 points of walking with intensity (with a brisk mentality)

POINT 1- Be doing God will. Jesus said to his parents at the age of 12. I must be about my fathers business. (Luke 2:49).

POINT 2-Don't procrastinate. Jesus said to his disciples I must work the work of him that sent me while it is day, the night comes when no one can work. (John 9:4).

POINT 3-Be prepared for battle. Put on the whole armor of God that you may withstand the wiles of the devil. (Ephesians 6:11).

POINT 4-Don't go to spiritual sleep. It's high time that we awake out of sleep for our salvation is nearer than when we believed. (Romans 13:11).

Get rid of weights and sins. Let us lay aside every weight and the sin which easily beset us and let us run the race with patience that is set before us. Looking to Jesus the author and finisher of our faith.)

MOVE MOUNTAIN, GET OUT OF MY WAY

The mountains in this context is not physical mountain like Mount Everest. Mountains in life can be hard to climb and difficult to get to the top of. Jesus told his disciples to speak to mountains and tell them be removed and thrown sea. With only needing faith as a grain of a mustard seed. (Mark 11:22) but let's not leave out that he said if we doubt not in our heart but believe those things you say will come to pass you will have whatever you say. Life and death lies within what we say. Power of life and death lies within the tongue. (Proverbs 18:21). I encourage you to speak to your mountains although you can't see them moving. We walk by faith and not by sight. 2 Corinthians 5:7). We should say as if they are already and out of our way.

HE BROUGHT YOU OUT TO HELP OTHERS OUT

I extend this message out to all the mothers across the world. Mothers go through a lot. Few days and full of trouble (Job14:1). When God bring you out it helps others to come. So continue to let your light shine that mankind will see your good work and glorify our father in Heaven. (Matthew 5:16). The mother in the Bible that couldn't have children (Hannah) cried out to God. (1 Samuel 1:1-20). The mother that refused to have her baby cut in half is a testament to you mothers today. (1 King 5:3-15). The mother giving her last to the man of God is a testimony to you mothers that will go to the bitter end to sacrifice on behalf of God. (1 Kings 17:8-24).

Receive His Peace, It Belongs To You Part 2

PART 2: Most of us if not all of us want to receive what belong to us. We however don't always go about the right way to receive the Peace that the Lord has for us that belong to us. The songwriter said O what PEACE we often forfeit O what needless pain we bear all because we do not carry everything to God in prayer ♪. It is the peace of God that keeps our hearts and minds through Jesus Christ (Philippians 4:7). We should let (allow) the peace of God to rule in our hearts (Colossians 3:15). How so Brother Pastor? By receiving the PEACE that belongs to you given by the PRINCE OF PEACE (Jesus Christ) (Isaiah 9:6).

Satan That Is Seeking To Devour You Is No Match For The Savior That Is Seeking To Deliver You

The Bible says we should be sober, be vigilant because your adversary the devil (the arch enemy of God) as a roaring lion walks about seeking who he can devour (to absorb the mind fully). (1Peter 5:8). He is no match for the savior (Jesus Christ). Jesus said all power in heaven and earth is given unto me (Matthew 28:18). No matter what he comes at you with be encouraged to know that Jesus causes us to always triumph. (1 Corinthians 2:14). He is wanting you to think he has the upper hand on you. I serve notice on you satan. That Greater is he that is within you (Jesus) than he that is in the world. (1 John 4:4).

COME CLOSER, YOU'VE GOTTEN TOO DISTANT FROM ME

We are in a worldwide pandemic and social distancing is wise to adhere to. We likewise would be wise to adhere to the spirit of God. They that have an ear let them hear what the spirit is saying to the church. (Revelations 2:29). The Lord desire us to come closer to him. He said draw near to him and he will draw near to us. (James 4:8). Charles McCoy posted an essential post saying: When the wolves come stay close to the shepherd. Jesus is the good shepherd and the good shepherd gave his life for the sheep . (John 10:11). Please LIKE, SHARE, and SUBSCRIBE free of charge.

GO TO THE ROCK

In times like these we are often left wondering where can I go? Who can I run to? Whitney Houston said it right when she said I go to the ROCK. The Rock is Jesus Christ. When your way gets heavy. Helen Miller said it well she said Jesus said you can lean on me. When your load get heavy and burdens are hard to bear. Jesus said come to me all that labor and are heavy laden and I will give you rest. (Matthew 11:28)

WE ARE LIVING IN AN HOUR WHERE WE ALL NEED TO BE FILLED WITH HOLY GHOST POWER

Apostle Paul spoke about the hour in which we are now In today. He said that in the last days perilous (dangerous) times will come. (2 Timothy 3:1). Jesus spoke about the hour in which we now live. Jesus said a sign of his coming and the end of the world. There will be wars and rumors of wars, earthquakes in different places. Famines and pestilences. (Matthew 24:6-15.) Paul knew the importance of being filled with the Holy Ghost. He was filled with Holy Ghost on a street called Straight. (Acts 9:17,18). He taught and preached about the importance of being filled with the Holy Ghost for this hour. Jesus himself was the Holy Ghost. He cried out with a loud voice. If anyone thirst let them come after me believe on me as the scripture says and out of your belly (innermost) shall flow rivers of living water. He was talking about his spirit for at the time the Holy Ghost was not yet given. (John 7:38).

LET'S RUN THIS RACE FROM A SAFE PLACE

This life and journey in which we are on is often called a race. It is vitally important as to where and how we run this race. Many start out swift and strong, but the race is not given to the swift, nor the battle to the strong. (Ecclesiastes 9:11). But to the one that endure till the end shall be saved. (Matthew 24:13). I encourage each of you to run this race from a safe place and that is with the ALMIGHTY !! He that dwell in the secret place of the most high (ALMIGHTY GOD) shall abide (remain) under the shadow of the Almighty (Psalms 91:1-10). The safest name to run this race is in the name (Authority, Character) of the Lord. The name of the Lord is a strong tower, the righteous run there in and they are safe. (Proverbs 18:10).

LET'S RUN THIS RACE FROM A SAFE PLACE PART 2

PART 2: Safety is important in this day and time in all our lives In the midst of a pandemic be encouraged to run this race from a safe place. We need not only know what to do to be in a safe place. We need to know what not to do. In PART 2: I will give 5 points as to what not to do.

POINT 1: Lean not to your own understanding but trust in the Lord. In all our ways acknowledge him and he will direct our path (Proverbs 3:5).

Point 2: Don't do it the way you 🤔think. Your thoughts are not his thoughts and his ways are not our ways. (Isaiah 55:8).

POINT 3: Don't get faint hearted. Let us not be weary in well doing for in due season we will reap if we faint not. Galatians 6:9).

POINT 4: Don't look 👀back. They that take hold to the Gospel plough and look back is not fit for the kingdom of God. (Luke 9:62).

POINT 5: Don't draw back. We are not of them that draw back (Hebrews 10:39)

LET'S RUN THIS RACE FROM A SAFE PLACE PART 3

PART3: In Part 2 we covered what we should not do in order to run this race from a safe place. In PART 3 we want to cover what we should do to run this race from a safe place.

POINT 1: Have faith. Faith comes by hearing and hearing by the word of God. (Romans 10:17). Faith is essential to being in a safe place in Jesus. Without faith it is impossible to please him (Hebrews 11:5,6). Whoever comes to God MUST believe (trust, rely) that he is and that he is a rewarder of them that diligently seek him.

POINT 2: Receive the Holy Ghost so you can have power within your safe place. After the Holy Ghost has come upon you, you will have POWER. (Acts 1:8).

POINT 3: Deny yourself. If anyone will be his disciple (follower, learner) they must deny themselves take up their own cross and follow him (Matthew 24:16)

POINT 4: Be led by the spirit. Many as be led by the spirit of God they are the sons of God. (Romans 8:14.

POINT 5: when your load gets heavy go to Jesus. Come to me all that labor and are heavy laden and I (Jesus) will give you rest (Matthew 11:28).

HOW PRECIOUS IS
HE TO YOU & I

When something or someone is PRECIOUS they are of great value and not to be wasted or treated carelessly. The question to the body of Christ and to the world 🌐as a whole is how PRECIOUS (Valuable) is Jesus to you and I. Please view this video in it's entirety to see the depiction of the hand sanitizer, the Lysol, and the disinfectant wipes and gather how Precious these items are to you and I. Afterward let us examine ourselves by asking ourselves how Precious (Valuable) Is Jesus to you and I. Is he PRECIOUS enough to seek first the Kingdom of God (Matthew 6:33). Is he PRECIOUS enough to follow peace with all mankind and holiness without no one will see the Lord. (Hebrews 12:14) Please LIKE, SHARE, and SUSCRIBE TO THIS YOUTUBE channel. Bless you all

HOW PRECIOUS IS HE
TO YOU & I PART 2

PART 2: Our subject matter is put in the form of a question and one that you and I should answer honestly within ourselves. The Bible says search the scriptures for in them (the scriptures) you think ☺you have eternal life these are they who testify of me (Jesus) (John 5:39). When he is PRECIOUS (of great value) to us we should have no issues in being his disciple (Follower, learner) Jesus said if anyone will be his disciple let them deny themselves, take up their cross and follow him (Matthew 16:24). Please Like, share, and subscribe free of charge 🙏.

LET JESUS HAVE YOU

The key ✐word in our lesson subject is LET (Which means to allow). If/when we let (allow) Jesus to have his way is when out of our bellies (innermost) will flow rivers of living water (Speaking of his spirit). John 7:38. The Lord has said and is still saying. If my people who are called by my name shall humble themselves and pray and seek my face and turn from their wicked ways then will we hear from heaven. He will heal the land and forgive their sin (2 Chronicles 7:14)

Sooner Or Later It Will Work In Your Favor

The Bible says Let (don't allow) us not be weary in well doing for in due season we will reap if we faint not (Galatians 6:9). Sooner or later it's going to work in your favor. In spite of all you been through, going through or what is on the horizon. Sooner or later it's going to work in your favor.

DON'T LET WHAT YOUR EYES SEE CAUSE YOU TO FORGET WHAT GOD HAS SAID

Greetings to all in the name of Jesus. The context of this lesson is when Adam and Eve let their eyes 👀see cause them to forget what God had said. The Bible says by one mans disobedience (Adam) many were made sinners. By one mans obedience (Jesus) shall many be made righteous.

Don't let what your eyes 👀see cause you to forget what God has said PART 1: Mankind has been letting their eyes 👀see cause them to forget what God has said since all the way back in the garden of Eden. Eve saw that the fruit was good for food and let it cause her to forget that God said do not eat from the tree 🌳in the midst/ middle of the garden. She ate and so did Adam who was with her. (Genesis 3:6). Samson the most strongest human of his time let his eyes see cause him to forget what was said he desired to have Delilah in spite of his parents telling him not to. (Judges 14:3-6). Ultimately it cost him his life. David a man after God's own heart let what his eyes see cause him to forget what God has when he walked out on the balcony and saw Bathsheba taking a bath 🛁. (2 Samuel 11:2) It's like he went from the Lord is my Shepherd and I shall not want (Psalms 23:1) to The Lord is my Shepherd and I see 👀what I want. May we all be careful to not let what our eyes see cause us to forget what God has said. Click on link below and push subscribe to this video and all of these YouTube videos free of charge. God bless you please share with others

DON'T LET WHAT YOUR EYES SEE CAUSE YOU TO FORGET WHAT GOD HAS SAID PART 2

Don't let what your eyes 👀see cause you to forget what God has said PART 2: Yesterday we pointed out how what we see can get us in 😖water 🐚with God, EXAMPLES: Adam and Eve, Samson, David. We should learn from our predecessors of the dangers of what we see can cause us to forget what God has said our eyes 👀will have us looking back. Remember Lots wife. (Luke 17:32) She looked back and turned to a pillar of salt 🧂 (Genesis 19:26). The eyes will have us in the world. The Bible says love not the world nor the things that are in the world (1John 2:15). Part of that come from the lust of the eye 👁). The Bible says if our eye 👁 offend (causes us to stumble) pluck it out for its better to enter the kingdom maimed than the whole body be cast into hell. (Matthew 5:29, Mark 9:47). Click on link below and subscribe free of charge. I will be honored that you share this gospel with others.

WHEN WE PREPARE FOR WHAT WE HAVE PRAYED- PART 1

In order to prepare for what we have prayed for there will be times it does not look like it's going to happen and that's when we must walk by faith and not by sight. (2 Corinthians 5:7). There will be times we must prepare even though it gets wearisome. Paul said let us not be weary in well doing for in due season we will reap if we faint not. (Galatians 6:9)

FROM DEPLETED TO COMPLETED

Our lesson text is centered around two words DEPLETED and COMPLETED. To be DEPLETED is to lack in number or quantity. To Be COMPLETED from the Bible perspective is to be made whole. Be encouraged to know that Jesus can take you from DEPLETED (lacking) to COMPLETED (made whole). He which has began a good work in you will perform (COMPLETE) it until the day of Jesus Christ. (Philippians 1:6).

WE GO FROM GLORY TO GLORY, NOT FROM PIT TO PIT

To go from glory to glory is to be continually changed into what we were created to be. God created us for his glory. Through him we go from glory to glory for we are fearfully and wonderfully made (Psalms 139:14). It is he (God) who made us and not we ourselves, we are his people and the sheep of his Pasture. Psalms 100:3).

When I Wanted To Give Up GOD Said Get Up

Perhaps you almost let go. You felt like you could not take life anymore. Depression had you down and satan had you bound. But God held you close so you wouldn't let go. Be encouraged everyone to not give up. Let us not be weary in well doing for in due season we will reap if we faint not. (Galatians 6:9). Get up even if you have to cry. For weeping may endure but a night, but joy comes in the morning. (Psalms 30:5). Get up in spite of the suffering. For if you suffer with him you will reign with him. (2 Timothy 2:12).

WHEN I WANTED TO GIVE UP
GOD SAID GET UP PART 2

Part 2: many have been at the point of throwing in the towel. Instead you Cast (Throw) all your cares upon him for he cares for you. (1 Peter 5:7). You wanted to give up feeling you had no one to look to. Yet you got up and looked to Jesus the author and finisher of your faith. (Hebrews 12:2). The devil saw you with your head down and thought he had you until he saw you look up and say AMEN!!

EVEN IN THIS HOUR THE WORD OF GOD STILL HAS POWER

Thou we are living in an hour where seemingly many do not let the word have free course. (2 Thessalonians 3:1). There are also those that cause the word of God to be of none effect (Mark 7:13).I stopped by to tell somebody today that the word of God is quick and powerful (Hebrews 4:12). It has the power as Jeremiah said it's like a hammer ✒that breaks the rocks in pieces (Jeremiah 23:29). The word has power as the psalmist has said it is a lamp to my feet 👣and a light 💡to my pathway (Psalms 119:105).

A Powerful Encounter That Produces A Powerful Change

The most/best encounter one will/can ever have is an encounter with Jesus Christ. The encounter will produce a powerful change and you will never be the same. If anyone be in Christ they are a new creation old things are passed away and behold all things are become new. (2 Corinthians 5:17)

LET'S BE AT THE TABLE TO SERVE THE ONE THAT IS ABLE

The motive in which we serve God or come in the presence of God is vitally important. All the ways of mankind are clean in his own eyes but the Lord weighs the spirit/ motive. (Proverbs 16:2). Make sure your motives are pure no matter how well it seems to you. There is a way that seems right unto mankind, but the end are the ways of death. (Proverbs 14:12).Grandma said whatsoever you do for Jesus let it be real. We are to serve him in sincerity and in truth. (Joshua 24:14). God is not a fairytale. God is a spirit and seek those to worship him. They that worship him must worship him in spirit and in truth. (John 4:24). Many are/ will be deceived in their servitude toward God. Jesus said everyone that says Lord Lord will not enter. (Matthew 7:21). Many will say in that day Lord have we not Prophesied in your name, and cast out devils in your name and done many wonderful works in your name. Then will I profess unto them I know you not for your works

WHILE YOU ARE GOING THROUGH, LET JESUS WORK ON YOU

While you are going through, not if you are going through or just in case you are going through for you are either going through, been through or as grandma said if you have not been through just keep on living. Job said one that is born of a woman is of few days and full of trouble. (Job 14:12). Since going through is a given we may as well let Jesus work on us. For it is God which works in you both to will and to do of his good pleasure. (Philippians 2:13). Now is the time to let Jesus work on us. Jesus at the age of 12 said I must be about my father's business. (Luke 2:49). He said I must work the works of him that sent me while it is day for the night come when no one can work. (John 9:4). It behooves (our responsibility) us to let Jesus work on us for the outward perish but the inward is renewed day by day(2 Corinthians 4:16). Every day he wake us is an opportunity to draw near to him and he will draw near to us. (James 4:8). I pray for everyone to allow Jesus to work on us with being confident of this very thing that he which has began a good in you will perform complete) it until the day of Jesus Christ. (Philippians 1:6).

Stay Connected To The Vine And You Will Be Just Fine

Jesus didn't just say he is a vine, he said he is the TRUE VINE. He told Thomas that I am the way, the truth and the life. (John 14:6). If/when we stay connected to him come what will or may we will be just fine. For all things work together for the good of them that love God and are the called according to his purpose. (Romans 8:28).

THEY WHO WORK BY THE POWER GET PAID BY THE POWER

Take note 📝 that the subject is not work by the hour nor get paid by the hour. When one work by the hour they can CLAIM their STEAK 🐾. When one work by the power they can STAKE their CLAIM.

LET'S TAKE OUR FAITH OUT OF MAN AND PLACE IT IN THE SAVIOR'S HANDS

The subject of our lesson title by no means belittle mankind. Mankind are to be kind to one another, tender hearted and forgiving one to another. (Ephesians 4:32). Mankind need each other because Iron sharpens Iron (Proverbs 27:17). Also we that are strong ought to bear the infirmities of the weak. (Romans 15:1). Reason being we should take our faith out of mankind is because of how mighty the savior is. Songwriter says heaven and earth ADORE him Angels bow BEFORE him. The bible says there is none beside him. (Deuteronomy 4:35). There is none like him. None we can compare him to. (Isaiah 40:18). No other can take 2 fishes, and 5 barley loaves of bread and feed a multitude of 5000 men not counting the women and children. (John 6:9). Our faith should be in the saviors hand for mankind look on the outer appearance but God (the savior) looks on the heart. (1 Samuel 16:7). Mankind may/ will tell you a lie. It is impossible for God to lie (Hebrews 6:18). He is not like mankind that he should lie nor is he the son of mankind that he should repent. Has he said and shall he not do it? Has he spoken and not make it good? (Numbers 23:19). Stay tuned for part 2 of: Let's take our faith out of MAN and place it in the Saviors HAND.

Let's Take Our Faith Out Of Man and Place It In The Savior's Hands Part 2

Part 2: In the context of this lesson the man with the infirmity for 38 years was dependent upon mankind to get help only to be let down. David said I will lift my eyes 👀to the hills from which comes my help my help comes from the Lord which made the heaven and earth. (Psalms 121:1). As long as he was looking to mankind he could/would render an excuse. When we place our faith in the savior hand we are without excuse. (Romans 1:20). Often times instead of placing our faith in the Savior hands we get like burger 🍔king wanting to have it our way and the way we think 🤔it should be. But your thoughts 💭are not his thoughts and your ways are not his ways. (Isaiah 55:8). If you don't place your faith in the saviors hand you will do what Proverbs said not to do. Lean not to your own understanding but trust in the Lord in all your ways acknowledge him and he will direct your path. (Proverbs 3:5).It behooves (our duty, responsibility)us to not put our faith in mankind for mankind has no heaven or hell to put us in. We should not fear mankind. Fear not the one that can kill the body fear the one that can kill the body and soul in Hell. (Luke 12:4). LETS TAKE OUR FAITH OUT OF MANKIND AND PLACE IT IN THE HANDS OF THE SAVIOR (JESUS CHRIST).

WE ARE GOING TO DO WHAT THEY SAID COULD NOT BE DONE PART 2

It has been well said that man's extremities (the furthest point or limit of something) is God's opportunity. For with mankind things are impossible, but with God all things are possible. (Matthew 19:26). No matter who said it can't be done, we should go with God who cannot lie. He is not a man that he should lie nor is he the son of mankind that he should repent. Has he not said and shall he not do it? Or has he spoken and shall he not do it? (Numbers 23:19). Perhaps you feel as though things are not seemingly holding you up. That's the time to know that he is able to keep you from falling and present you faultless before the presence of his glory with exceeding joy. (Jude 1:24). If you are in utter despair. He is able to save to the uttermost them that come unto God by him. (Hebrews 7:25). It may not look like it can't be done but we walk by faith and not by sight. (2 Corinthians 5:7). Reason being not because we are able but because he is able to do exceedingly abundantly above all that we ask or think 😊 according to the power that works within us. (Ephesians 3:20).

WE ARE GOING TO DO WHAT THEY SAID COULD NOT BE DONE PART 3

Many bible patriarchs went against the grain and did what others said could not be done David slew the giant Goliath. (1 Samuel 17:1). We too can overcome our giants. For we are more than a conqueror through him that loved us. (Romans 8:37). We do what they said can't be done through Jesus Christ. The Joy of the Lord is our strength. (Nehemiah 8:10). Paul said I can do all things not through himself but through Christ which strengthens me. (Philippians 4:13). We can do what they said can't be done so therefore let us not be weary in well doing for in due season we will reap if we faint not. (Galatians 6:9). We can do it in spite of the plans, schemes of others. No weapon formed against you shall prosper. (Isaiah 54:17). We can do what they said can't be done when we have the greater one (Jesus Christ). For greater is he that is within you than he that is within the world. (1 John 4:4). We can do what they said can't be done even when the enemy comes in like a flood the spirit of the Lord will lift up a standard against him. (Isaiah 59:19).

WHAT DO I DO TO GET THROUGH WHAT I AM GOING THROUGH

After we come to a conclusion that we are going to go through things in life. Job said one that is born of a woman is of few days and full of trouble. (Job 14:12). We find ourselves asking what can we do to get through what we are going through? For one we need faith to get through. Faith comes by hearing and hearing by the word of God. (Romans 10:17). Jesus said if you have faith as a grain of mustard seed you can speak to mountains and tell them to move and go yonder place. If you doubt not in your heart but believe those things you say shall come to pass you will have whatever you say. (Mark 11:22-24). Faith is essential to getting through what you are going through. For without faith it is impossible to please him. Whoever comes to God must believe that he is and that he is a rewarder of them which diligently seek him. (Hebrews 11:5-6). We should have faith even when we cannot see our way through. For we walk by faith and not by sight. (2 Corinthians 5:7). When you are going through sometimes the load is heavy and burdens are hard to bear. Jesus says come to me all who labor and are heavy laden and I will give you rest. (Matthew 11:28). I close today by saying let us not be weary in well doing for in due season we will reap if we faint not. (Galatians 6:9).

JESUS PAID THE PRICE & LET US KEEP THE CHANGE

Our subject title reminds me of when I was a little boy and my mom would send me to the store and after paying the price for what she wanted, every now and then she would let her child keep the change. That doesn't compare to the price that Jesus paid when he shed his blood for us. For without the shedding of blood there is no remission (removal) of our sins. (Hebrews 9:22). Not only did he pay the price, he also let his child keep the change. The change I kept from mom May have been $3.16 cents. But the change from Jesus was John 3:16. For God so loved the world that he gave his only begotten son that whoever believes in him should not perish but have everlasting life. The change he let us keep is a changed life. We keep the change when we get in Christ. Therefore if anyone be in Christ they are a new creation old things are passed away and behold all things are become new. (2 Corinthians 5:17). We keep the change as the outward perish but the inward man is renewed day by day. (2 Corinthians 4:16). Jesus paid it all and the songwriter says all to him I owe, my sin was crimsoned stained he washed them white as snow. He paid a debt he did not owe we owed a debt we could not pay. Thank you Jesus for paying the price for the wages of sin is death but the gift of God is eternal life. (Romans 6:23). Thank you Jesus for paying the price for without you we could do nothing. (John 15:5). May we realize that because he paid the price. We are not our own but we are bought with a price. (1 Corinthians 6:20). May we know that we were not redeemed with corruptible things like silver and gold from our vain traditions, but by the precious blood of Christ. (1 Peter 1:18).

Jesus Paid the Price & Let Us Keep the Change Part 2

Part 2: My friend Nicola McFadden pointed out that the change we keep is a changed life. Therefore if anyone be in Christ they are a new creation old things are passed away and behold all things are become new. (2, Corinthians 5:17). The change we keep is a changed mindset. Paul said let this mind be in you that was also in Christ Jesus. (Philippians 2:5).The change we keep is a changed heart. I will take out the stony heart and put in a heart of flesh (Ezekiel 36:26). May we be determined to keep the change of a new identity for you are not your own but you are bought with a price. (1 Corinthians 6:20).There are many that do not take advantage of keeping the change. Jesus came in the world and the world knew him not, he came to his own and his own received him not. But to many as received him to them he gave power (the right) to become the sons/daughters of God. (John 1:12). The price Jesus paid can/will allow us to have life and life more abundantly. (John 10:10).

FROM SELECTION TO DIRECTION

The same God that select us also direct us. Therefore you must not lean to your own understanding but trust in the Lord with all your heart and acknowledge him in all your ways and he will direct your path. (Proverbs 3:5). To be a disciple (follower) of Christ we must have direction. If anyone will be his disciple they must deny themselves take up their cross and follow him. (Matthew 16:24). To go in right direction we must understand that our thoughts are not his thoughts and our ways are not his ways. (Isaiah 55:8). When going in the direction he will have us to go we can't be like burger king. We are not going to have it our way. From selection to direction we can't do it the way that seems right. There is a way that seems right unto a person but the end are the ways of death (Proverbs 14:12). God directs through his word. He said abide (remain in me and my word in you and you can ask what you will and it shall be done. (John 15:4). When God directs he said that a good person steps are ordered by him. (Psalms 37:23). The Lord directs by his spirit. Many as be led of the spirit they are the sons/daughters of God. (Romans 8:14).

FROM SELECTION TO DIRECTION PART 2

PART2: In life we both spiritual and natural we need DIRECTION. Those that Jesus selected also followed directions. Before he sent the Holy Ghost he left direction. He told them to go to Jerusalem and stay there till they be endued (clothed) with power from on high. (LUKE 24:49). When the Lord gives direction he has a purpose for giving it. He said after the Holy Ghost was come upon them they would receive power and be witnesses (PURPOSE). (ACTS 1:8) When Peter preached and the house of Israel was pricked (convicted) in their heart they said men and brethren what must we do (DIRECTION) Peter said repent (become Godly sorrowful, turn, change) and be baptized (immersed) in the name (AUTHORITY, CHARACTER) Lord Jesus Christ for the remission (removal) of your sins and you shall receive the gift of the Holy Ghost. (ACTS 2:38). Following direction after being selected is essential to us. For Direction we should follow route 66 (The word of God. Paul said study 📖to show yourself approved unto God, a workman that need not to be ashamed rightly dividing the word of truth. (2 Timothy 2:15). I pray we all have the mindset to take up our cross and follow him. (Matthew 16:24).

GO AFTER THE LIFE YOU HAVE PRAYED FOR

I for one have prayed for a life. I also for one have been guilty of not going after the life I prayed for. Jesus said seek and we shall find. (Matthew 7:7). We should have faith to go after the life we have prayed for. For without faith it is impossible to please God. Whoever comes to God must believe that he is and that he is a rewarder of them which diligently seek him. (Hebrews 11:5-6). We must act upon our faith to have the life we have prayed for. For faith without works is dead. (James 2:26). The Bible says when we pray we are to believe and we shall receive. (Mark 11:24). When we pray for a life it is important that we cast (throw) not away our confidence which has a great recompense of reward. (Hebrews 10:35). When going after the life you prayed for don't draw back for we are not of them which draw back but of them which believe to the saving of the soul. (Hebrews 10:39). May we all be like Paul and go after the life we have prayed for. By pressing towards the mark of the high calling of God which is in Christ Jesus. (Philippians 3:14).

GO AFTER THE LIFE YOU HAVE PRAYED FOR PART 2

Part 2: There are ways in which to go after the life we have prayed for. One way is to be obedient. Obedience is better than sacrifice (1Samuel 15:22). If we would obey and hearken diligently to his voice he will command his blessings upon us and cause them to overtake us (Deuteronomy 28:1-14). We can have what we pray for if we abide (remain)in him and his word in us we can ask what we will and it shall be done. (John 15:7).We can have what we pray for when we receive with meekness the engrafted (implanted) word which is able to save your souls. But it's not enough to just hear it and have what we pray for. Be you doers of his word and not hearers only. If anyone hear the word and not a doer they are like one looking at their face in the mirror and turning away and forgetting the manner of person they were. When we are a doer and not a forgetful hearer we will be blessed in our deeds. (James 1:22). We got God for with God all things are possible. (Matthew 19:26). We got Emmanuel (God with us (Matthew 1:23). We got the word that won't come back void. (Isaiah 55:11). We have the Holy Ghost. He will bring all things to our remembrance (John 14:26). We have Jesus who will never leave us or forsake us. (Hebrews 13:5). Therefore we can/should go after the life we have prayed for.

LET'S DO OURSELVES A FAVOR BY MAKING ROOM FOR THE SAVIOR

One of the greatest favors we can do for ourselves is to make room for the savior (Jesus Christ). For one he himself said that without me you could do nothing. (John 15:5). When we make room for him we cause the thief to not achieve what he is after. For the thief comes but for to steal to kill and to destroy. Jesus said I am come that you might have life and life more abundantly. (John 10:10). They had no room for Jesus in the Inn. We can ill afford to not have room for him in our daily lives. Jesus said if anyone will be his disciple (Follower) let them deny themselves take up their cross and follow him. (Matthew 16:24). We do ourselves a favor by having him for he is the great Emmanuel which being interpreted is God with us. I pray for the world ⊕to make room for the savior. For Jesus is the answer for the world TODAY. Above him there's no other Jesus is the WAY! Please click on the link below hit subscribe free of charge. Please share with others for they who share with others shall themselves be blessed.

LET'S FOCUS ON THE PROMISE

By no means are we exempt from problems. Job said that one that is born of a woman is of few days and full of trouble. (Job 14:1) What we must learn to do is to not focus on the problem but focus on the promise. For every problem you encounter there is a promise to overcome it. Don't focus on the trouble focus on the promise to your trouble. For God is our refuge and strength a very present help in trouble. (Psalms 46:1). Perhaps you are facing many afflictions yet you should focus on the promise. Many are the afflictions of the righteous but God delivers them out of them all. (Psalms 34:19). You are being persecuted and that is a problem for he that live Godly in Christ Jesus shall suffer persecution. (2 Timothy 2:12). We are persecuted but not forsaken. (2 Corinthians 4:9). Jesus promised to never leave us or forsake us. He said I will be with you always even to the end of the world. (Matthew 28:20). David focused on the promise and said I was young and now am old yet have I never seen the righteous forsaken or their seed begging bread. (Psalms 37:25).

PLACED IN A POSITION OF VICTORY, SO THAT WE CAN WALK IN VICTORY

By the Grace of God all mankind has the opportunity to be placed in a position of victory through Christ Jesus. For by grace (God's unmerited favor) are you saved through faith, not of works, not of ourselves, unless anyone would boast. It is the gift of God. (Ephesians 2:8-9). We are placed in a position of victory not by works of righteousness which we have done but according to his mercy he saved us by the washing and regeneration of the Holy Ghost. (Titus 3:5). Not that the devil is out to convince you that you are not in a position of victory. For he is the accuser of the brethren. (Revelation 12:10). Be encouraged to know that there is therefore now no condemnation of them which are in Christ Jesus, who walk not after the flesh but after the spirit. (Romans 8:1). I pray that all not be discouraged of setbacks in your life. Be confident of this very thing that he which has began a good in you will perform it until the day of Jesus Christ. (Philippians 1:6). When one is in a place of victory the enemy may come in like a flood but the spirit of the Lord will lift up a standard against him. (Isaiah 59:19). Placed in a position of victory the world can't do you no harm. For greater is he that is within you than he that is in the world. (1 John 4:4).

THE LORD IS TRUE TO FORM & WILL LET YOU RIDE OUT THE STORM

There is no greater one to ride out the storm ☁with than the one that is true to form. (Jesus Christ). He is the true light. (John 1:9). He is the true vine (John 15:1) He is the way the truth and the life. (John 14:6). Since we all at some time or another will go through a storm ☁. We should make sure he is on board with us. For Jesus said that without me you could do nothing (John 15:5). Jesus awoke out of sleep ☺and spoke to the wind 🌬 and the wind ceased (stopped). He spoke to the sea 🌊and said peace be still. They looked at one another and said what manner (kind) of man is this that even the wind 🌬and the sea 🌊obey him. (Mark 4:39). With the Lord on the inside of us we can ride out the storm. For greater is he that is within you than he that is within the world. (John 4:4).

THE LORD IS TRUE TO FORM & WILL LET YOU RIDE OUT THE STORM PART 2

PART 2: Most of us if not all of us have either been in a storm. Just come out of a storm 🐾or perhaps you are in a storm ⛆right now. Being a child of God does not exempt us from the storms of life. Many are the afflictions of the righteous. You can yet ride out the storm, for God delivers them out of them all. (Psalms 34:19). We can encounter storms through other people. He that live Godly in Christ Jesus shall suffer persecution. (2 Timothy 3:12). Even through persecution you can ride out the storm. We are persecuted but not forsaken. Cast down but not destroyed (2 Corinthians 4:9). Paul was one that rode out many storms. How did he do it? For one he said nothing shall be able to separate us from the love of God. (Romans 8:35). He also said he was forgetting those things which are behind and reaching forth to those things before him. I press toward the mark of the high calling of God which is in Christ Jesus. (Philippians 3:14). May we all be encouraged to ride out the storm. You can do it. Paul said I can do all things through Christ which strengthens me. (Philippians 4:13).

THE LORD IS TRUE TO FORM & WILL LET YOU RIDE OUT THE STORM PART 3

To be true to form is to do what's expected based on past experience. Based on past experience Jesus Christ is the same yesterday, today and forevermore (Hebrews 13:8). Perhaps you are in a storm in your life and wonder how can you ride it out. You ride it out by trusting in him that is true to form he cannot lie. He is not a man that he should lie nor is he the son of mankind that he should repent. Has he said and shall he not do it. Has he spoken and not make it good. (Numbers 23:19). He is true to form. Isaiah said his word has gone forth out of his mouth and will not return to him void (empty). (Isaiah 55:11). You can ride out the storm for he is true to form and will never leave you or forsake you. He has declared that I am with you always even to the end of the world (Matthew 28:19). David said it like this. I was young and now am old yet have I never seen the righteous forsaken or their seed begging bread. (Psalms 37:25). The lord is true to form in the midst of your tears. For they that sow in tears shall reap in joy (Psalms 126:5). Weeping may endure for a night but joy comes in the morning. (Psalms 30:5). May we let the peace of God rule in our hearts. (Colossians 3:15).

I Need To Know So That I Can Grow, & Not Be A Show

In order to grow in Christ we are going to need to know how to grow. My people are destroyed for the lack of knowledge. (Hosea 4:6). God has granted us ways to have the knowledge it takes to grow. He said behold I give to you Pastors according to my heart which will feed you with knowledge and understanding. (Jeremiah 3:15). That's one way we can grow. Another way to grow. Jesus said you shall know the truth and the truth will make you free. (John 8:32). Another way to grow is to study to show yourselves approved to God, a workman that need not to be ashamed rightly dividing the word of truth. (2 Timothy 2:15). We can know and grow by having faith. Faith comes by hearing and hearing by the word of God. (Romans 10:17).We can know and grow when we hear what the spirit says to the church .(Revelations 2:29).

You Are GOD Made, Now Are You Ready For An Upgrade

The scripture support that we all are God made. The Lord God formed man of the dust of the ground, breathed into his nostrils ♌the breath of life and man became a living soul. (Genesis 2:7).After he had made everything good he said let us make man in our image and in our likeness. (Genesis 1:26). We are made by God. In other words the stork didn't bring us nor did we make ourselves. Know you not that it is he that made us and not we ourselves. We are his people and the sheep of his Pasture. (Psalms 100:3). When God made you he didn't make any junk. Regardless of what others say to you or about you. You are fearfully and wonderfully made. (Psalms 139:14). People may take you for granted. But because you are God made I encourage you to not be weary in well doing for in due season you will reap if you faint not. (Galatians 6:9). When you are God made and not where you want/ need/ ought to be. Be confident of this very thing that he which has began a good work in you will perform (complete)it until the day of Jesus Christ. (Philippians 1:6). Stay tuned tomorrow for Part 2 of You are God made now are you ready for an upgrade.

YOU ARE GOD MADE, NOW ARE YOU READY FOR AN UPGRADE PART 2

PART 2: The God of Abraham, Isaac and Jacob that made us want us to be made whole. Paul said be confident of this very thing that he which has began a good work in you will perform (complete) it until the day of Jesus Christ. (Philippians 1:6). We are God made not just to merely exist but we are made to have life and life more abundantly. (John 10:10).God made us to have good success. (Joshua 1:8). He didn't make us to fail. He said I know the thoughts 🗨I have towards you. Thoughts 🗨of Peace and not evil to give you an expected end (a hopeful future). (Jeremiah 29:11). His desire is that we prosper and be in health even as our soul shall prosper. (3 John 1:2). He made us and promised to never leave us or forsake us. (Hebrews 13:5). Be encouraged everyone for the God that made us will be with us always even to the end of the world. (Matthew 28:19-20). David said I was young and now am old yet have I never seen the righteous forsaken or their seed begging ☹bread 🍞.(Psalms 37:25).

YOU ARE GOD MADE, NOW ARE YOU READY FOR AN UPGRADE PART 4

PART 4: God made the World and God made us. The earth is the Lords, the world 🌍and they (you and I) that dwell there in. (Psalms 24:1). We are all his by creation. It should therefore behoove (our duty or responsibility) to be his by redemption. By being born again (John 3:5). We that are his by redemption (Purchased by his blood) ought to also tell all those that are God made about the savior (Jesus Christ). Let the redeemed (those that are bought with a price) say so who has been redeemed from the hand of the enemy (satan). (Psalms 107:1). We are God made and when we accept Christ he changes us. Therefore if anyone be in Christ he is a new creation. Old things are passed away and behold all things are become new. (2 Corinthians 5:17). We are not our own but bought with a price. (1 Corinthians 6:20). May we take advantage of Christ coming into this world 🌍to save sinners (you and I). (1 Timothy 1:15). For how shall we escape if we neglect so great a salvation. (Hebrews 2:3). May we keep in remembrance all the benefits of belonging to him. Bless the Lord O my soul. And forget none of his benefits. Who heals all of our diseases, who forgives all our iniquities. (Psalms 103:1).

You Are God Made, Now Are You Ready For An Upgrade Part 5

Part 5: In part 1-4 we discussed of being God made for he made us and not we ourselves (Psalms 100:3). We now pose a question: Are you ready for an upgrade? To upgrade is to raise to a higher standard. We know that faith comes by hearing and hearing by the word of God. (Romans 10:17). Let's add to faith virtue (strength). That's an upgrade and we are going to need it. For the Joy of the Lord is our strength. (Nehemiah 8:10). We are to add to virtue knowledge. That's an upgrade for my people perish for the lack of knowledge. (Hosea 4:6). We add to knowledge temperance (self control). Jesus is the supreme example of self control. When he was reviled he didn't revile back. (1 Peter 2:23). When we get to where we love our enemies then we can say that we have upgraded (Matthew 5:44). We add to temperance patience that is indeed an upgrade. For with patience we possess (control) our soul. (Luke 21:19). We must let (allow) patience to have its perfect work. (James 1:4). May we all continue to strive for upgrades (raise to a higher standard) In Jesus Name Amen 🎵.

YOU ARE GOD MADE, NOW ARE YOU READY FOR AN UPGRADE PART 6

PART 6: We have all voluntarily or involuntarily have experienced upgrades in our natural lives. Example: I recall as a kid seeing an 8 track player, we have upgraded from an 8 track player to a DVD ⊙player. Likewise in the spirit realm we can go from like a baby that desires the sincere milk of the word. (1 Peter 2:2) We can now upgrade from milk to the meat of the word. (1 Corinthians 3:2). We can upgrade from an eye ◉for an eye, from a tooth ♪for a tooth. (Exodus 21:24). To love our enemies and pray for them which despite fully use us. (Luke 6:27). We can upgrade from fighting our battles to realizing that the battle is not yours but belong to the Lord. (2 Chronicles 20:15). We upgrade from a burger 🍔king mentality of have it your way to your way are not his way and his thoughts are not your thoughts. (Isaiah 55:8). Be encouraged everyone to examine areas of your life where you see the need for an upgrade. Be rest assured we all have areas of improvement. We are going to need upgrade until he says well done you good and faithful servant. (Matthew 25:21).

THE BALL IS IN YOUR COURT

The ball is in your court is a sports term meaning it's your serve now. On the spiritual side of life it's our serve now. God has given us all that pertain to life and Godliness, the ball is now in our court. (2 Peter 1:3). Jesus Christ came into the world to save sinners. (1 Timothy 1:15) he did that the ball is in our court. He came to seek and to save that which is lost. (Luke 19:10) He did that the ball is now in our court. He came that we might have life and life more abundantly. (John 10:10). He made a way for us to have abundant life. The ball is now in our court. He shedded blood for the remission (removal) of our sins which without there would be no remission (removal). (Hebrews 9:22). The ball is in our court. He died to die no more. The ball is now in our court. May we all be like Joshua and say as for me and my house we will serve the Lord. (Joshua 24:15). May we all take heed to the words of Christ. God is a spirit and seek such to worship him they that worship him must worship him in spirit and in truth. (John 4:23-24). The ball is in our court.

THE BALL IS IN YOUR COURT PART 2

PART 2: The ball is in our court to receive all that God has for us. God has exceeding and great precious promises for us. (2 Peter 1:4). He will show you things that you know not (Jeremiah 33:3). For eye 👁 has not seen nor ear 👂heard neither has it entered into the heart ♥of mankind what the Lord has prepared for them that love him. (1 Corinthians 2:9). When the ball is in our court and we have not still received. The writer says we have not because we ask not. Then when we ask we ask amiss (Aimlessly). (James 4:2). The ball is in our court but we also must have our priorities in order. Yes we need this and we need that to make it in everyday life. The Father knows what we have need of even before we ask. (Luke 12:30). The ball is in our court to use priorities. That is we seek first the kingdom of God (God's way of doing things) and his righteousness and all these things will added unto you. (Luke 6:33). Jesus said no one having denied themselves shall in this life land, 🏠houses, and in the world to come Eternal life. (Luke 18:30). The ball is in our court. May we deny ourselves take up his cross and follow him. (Matthew 16:24).

WHAT ARE WE DOING WITH WHAT GOD HAS GIVEN US?

The Bible says that God has given us all things that pertain to life and Godliness (2 Peter 1:3). He has provided us all we need to make it in this life. The question is what are we doing with what God has given us. He has given us a plan of salvation. Whoever believes on him should not perish but have everlasting life. (John 3:16). We need to take advantage of his salvation plan. How shall we escape if we neglect so great (wonderful) a salvation? (Hebrews 2:3).What are we doing with our lives he has given us. He said above all I would that you prosper and be in health even as your soul prospers. (3 John 1:2). Life begins and end with Christ. Jesus said to Thomas: I am the way the truth and the life, no one comes to the father but by me. (John 14:6). Life is there for the taking when we choose Jesus. He said I am come that you might have life and life more abundantly. (John 10:10).

WILL YOU AIM TO PLEASE GOD?

When we make it our aim to please God we can be rest assured that there is no good thing he will withhold from them that walk uprightly. (Psalms 84:11). We aim to please him by seeking him and seeking after that which pleases him. If we seek we will find. (Matthew 7:7). We are pleasing to God when we delight (do that which brings pleasure) ourselves also in him and he will give us the desires of your heart. (Psalms 37:4). When we aim to please him others may take you for granted but let us not be weary in well doing for in due season we will reap if we faint not. (Galatians 6:9).If we make it our aim to please him I hear David saying I was young and now am old yet have I never seen the righteous forsaken or his seed begging . (Psalms 37:25).That's enough in itself for us all to aim to please him not to mention that he will supply all your needs according to his riches in glory by Christ Jesus.(Philippians 4:19).

GOD WILL STRAIGHTEN IT OUT

There are things we need straightened out in our lives. I Stopped by YouTube today to tell someone that God will straighten it out. If you are facing some crooked turns in your life. He will make crooked places straight. If you are going through a rough time . He will make rough places smooth. (Isaiah 40:4). Perhaps you need something straightened out right now. God is our refuge and strength a very present help in trouble. (Psalms 46:1). When your load gets heavy and burdens are hard to bear. Jesus said come to me all who labor and are heavy laden and I will give you rest. (Matthew 11:28). If you are going through one thing after another be not dismayed (distressed) whatever betide (happens, occurs) you. God will take care of you. For when the enemy shall come in like a flood the spirit of the Lord will lift up a standard against it (Isaiah 59:19).

GOD WILL STRAIGHTEN IT OUT PART 2

PART2: Whatever you are going through. God is able to straighten it out. If you are in need of salvation (deliverance). God is able to save to the uttermost all that come unto God by him. (Hebrews 7:25).If you are losing hope and falling by the way side. He is able to keep you from falling and present you faultless before his presence with exceeding joy. (Jude 1:24). God can/ will straighten it out. He is able to do exceedingly abundantly above all that we can ask or 😄💭think. (Ephesians 3:20). There is nothing too hard for God (Genesis 18:14). With God all things are possible (Matthew 19:26). Whatever you need him to straighten out for you he said cast all your care upon him for he cares for you.(1 Peter 5:7).

WE CAN BE AT EASE WHEN GOD IS WELL PLEASED

Oh! how we would love to be at ease (free from worry, relaxed). God has provided a way that we can be at ease. Therefore our aim should be to make him well pleased (Gratified, satisfied). When our ways please him he will make even our enemies to be at peace with us. (Proverbs 16:7). We can be at ease but there are some things that must be at place in our lives for God to be well pleased. We must have faith. For without faith it is impossible to please God, one that comes to God must believe that he is and that he is a rewarder of them which diligently seek him (Hebrews 11:5-6). We can be at ease but we must walk after the spirit and not after the flesh. For we cannot please God in the flesh. (Romans 8:8). We can be at ease when we cast all our care upon him for he cares for us. (1 Peter 5:7). Your load may be heavy and your burdens are hard to bear. Yet you can be at ease and God well pleased. Jesus said come to me all who labor and are heavy laden and I will give you rest. (Matthew 11:28). God is well pleased when we trust him. Lean not to your own understanding but trust in the Lord, in all your ways acknowledge him and he will direct your path. (Proverbs 3:5).

WE CAN BE AT EASE WHEN GOD IS WELL PLEASED PART 2

PART 2: The supreme example of pleasing God is the life of Jesus Christ. When John baptized him in the river of Jordan. God said this is my beloved son in who I am well pleased (Matthew 3:17). At the age of 12 he did what well pleased God. He said I must be about my father's business. (Luke 2:49). He showed us how to well please God by serving, not being served. He said I didn't come to be ministered (be served) to but to minister (To serve) and to give my life as a ransom to many. (Mark 10:45). At the Garden of Gethesemene he was still well pleasing to God. He said Father if it be your will let this cup (bitter cup of suffering) pass from me. Nevertheless not as I will but let your will be done. (Luke 22:42). I pray we all take lessons from the life of Jesus Christ that we may be at ease when God is well pleased.

FROM REJECTION TO SELECTION

Our subject matter is centered around 2 words. REJECTION and SELECTION. REJECTION means to be dismissed, no acceptance. When one is REJECTED it doesn't leave you feeling like James Brown 🎵. You are not left feeling good. When one is SELECTED you feel like James Brown you feel good. Jesus Christ can relate to how we feel when we are REJECTED. In all points he was tempted as you and I. Difference being he did it without sinning. (Hebrews 4:15). He did no sin. There was no guile (deceit) found in his mouth. (1 Peter 2:22). Jesus suffered for us in the flesh and told us to arm ourselves likewise. (1 Peter 4:1). We deal with rejection by having the same mind as he has. Let this mind be in you that was also in Christ Jesus. (Philippians 2:5). We like Jesus will suffer much for his namesake. (Acts 9:16). Yet I hear Paul saying that the suffering of this present time are not worthy to be compared to the glory that is going to be revealed in us. (Romans 8:18). You may have been rejected but I prophecy to someone today that eye 👁 have not seen nor ear 👂heard neither has it entered in the heart ♥of mankind what the Lord has prepared for them that love him. (1 Corinthians 2:9). In spite of your REJECTION you have been SELECTED. Selected by the one who will never leave you or forsake you. (Matthew 28:19). Selected by the one who causes us to always triumph. (2 Corinthians 2:14).

From Rejection To Selection Part 2

PART 2: We like Jesus May be despised and rejected (Dismissed) of mankind. (Isaiah 53:3). We are yet selected by God. You are a chosen (selected) generation, a royal 👑priesthood, a peculiar people that should show forth the praises of him who has called you out of darkness into his marvelous light. (1 Peter 2:9). Thou rejected you have been selected by God and you are fearfully and wonderfully made. (Psalms 139:14). Don't worry about those that rejected you they didn't make you as a matter of fact we didn't make ourselves. Know you not it is he (God) that made us and not we ourselves. We are his people and the sheep 🐑of his Pasture. (Psalms 100:3) The same God that allowed the rejection has selected you as Heirs with God and joint heirs with Christ. (Romans 8:17). You may be killed all the day long and accounted as sheep 🐑for the slaughter but nay (nevertheless) in all things we are more than a conqueror through him (Jesus) that love us. (Romans 8:36-38).

FROM REJECTION TO SELECTION PART 3

Part 3: We greet you in the immaculate (Perfectly clean, spotless) Name of Jesus. It is a great honor to be selected (chosen) by the one called Emmanuel (God with us. (Matthew 1:23). You don't and won't be perfect for him to select you. Jesus said to the young rich ruler there is none good but God (Mark 10:18). Isaiah was selected in spite of having unclean lips 𝒪. God said who shall I send and who will go for us. Isaiah said here am I send me. (Isaiah 6:8). Zacchaeus was a tax collector yet he was selected by Jesus as he told him to make haste (hurry up) and come down out of the sycamore tree. (Luke 19:5). Perhaps he is selecting someone reading 📖this post this morning will you be as Isaiah and say here am I Lord send me I will go. Perhaps someone reading 📖this post Jesus is selecting to come down. Will you be as Zacchaeus and make haste (hurry up) and come down? The day is coming for each of us to give in account to being selected/ called by God. He has called us with a Holy calling. (Timothy 1:9). God has highly exalted him and given him a name above every name that at the name of Jesus every knee shall bow and that every tongue ℧ shall confess that he (Jesus Christ) is Lord. (Philippians 2:10).

YOU CAN GET TO THE NEXT CHAPTER IN YOUR LIFE WHEN YOU KNOW THE AUTHOR OF YOUR LIFE

Knowing the author of our life is a key *element in getting to the next chapter in our life. Paul said in order to run *this race effectively. We are to lay aside every weight and the sin which does so easily beset (Throws you off) us and let us run *the race with patience that is set before us. We obtain that and get to the next chapter by looking to Jesus the author and finisher of our faith. (Hebrews 12:2) . Confidence is a key *element in getting to the next chapter. Be confident of this very thing that he who has began a good work in you will perform (Complete) it until the day of Jesus Christ. (Philippians 1:6). This is the confidence (Assurance) that we have in him. That if we ask anything according to his will, he hears *us, we do know that if he hears *us we have the petitions desired of him. (1 John 5:15). To get to the next chapter we are urged to not cast (throw) away our confidence for it has a great recompense of reward. (Hebrews 10:35). May we all know the Author (Jesus Christ) that we may get to the next chapter in our life.

YOU CAN GET TO THE NEXT CHAPTER IN YOUR LIFE WHEN YOU KNOW THE AUTHOR OF YOUR LIFE PART 2

PART 2: Getting to the next chapter in our lives can/will be challenging. The challenge is far more possible when we know the author (Jesus Christ). For with him all things are possible. (Mark 10:27). As the Author and finisher of our faith (Hebrews 12:2) He will never leave us or forsake us. He declared that I will be with you always even to the end of the world. (Matthew 28:19). David said it like this I was young but now am old yet have I never seen the righteous forsaken or their seed begging for bread 📖. (Psalms 37:25). When Jesus was coming to the coast of Caesarea Philipi, He asked his disciples Who do mankind say that I the son of man am? They said some say you are Elijah, some say Jeremiah, or one of the prophets, he then asked them who do you say that I am? Peter said that you are the Christ (Anointed one) the son of the living God. The Author and finisher of our faith has declared to you and I that upon this rock (This truth) Will I build my church 🏛️and the gates of hell shall not prevail against it.

YOU CAN GET TO THE NEXT CHAPTER IN YOUR LIFE WHEN YOU KNOW THE AUTHOR OF YOUR LIFE PART 4

Life is like a book 📖some chapters are exciting 😍,some are sad 😢, some are intriguing 👥🤔💬. In life we have to turn the page to get to the next chapter. We can get to the next chapter when we know the author. When Jesus asked his disciples who do mankind say that I am? Peter said you are the Christ (Anointed one) the son of the living God. David knew who the author was. He said I will lift my eyes 👀to the hills from where my help comes my help comes from the Lord who made the heaven and earth. In all that Job was going through he knew who is author was . He said thou he slay me yet will I trust him. Paul knew who the author was and encouraged us to look 👀to Jesus the author and finisher of our faith. Do you know him? Have you tried him? He will get us to the next chapter in our life.

WE HAVE TO GROW BEYOND TO GO BEYOND

By study ▭ of the word of God I am learning that in order to grow beyond some things I had to be willing to go beyond some things. The bible compares growing to a little baby 👶. Saying : Desire the sincere milk 🥛 of the word as newborn babies that you may grow thereby. We don't grow by seniority or by merit. We grow in grace and in the knowledge of the Lord Jesus Christ. Paul had to grow beyond in order to go beyond. He said when I was a child I thought 💬 as a child. I spoke as a child I did childish things. But when I became a man I put away childish things. He said not that I am already perfect neither have I apprehended all. But this one thing I do, I'm forgetting those things which are behind and I am reaching for those things that are before me. I press toward the mark of the high calling of God which is in Christ Jesus. May we all be determined to grow beyond that we may go beyond.

LET'S GO WITH THE MAN THAT HAS THE RIGHT PLAN

On the natural side of life there are many plans. Because many plans have affect on our lives we try to go with the one/ person that has our best interests at heart. Nationwide says we are on your side. On the Spiritual side of life David said the Lord is on my side. Prudential says get a piece of the rock. David says when my heart overwhelm me lead me to the rock that is higher than I. Allstate says you are in good hands with them. Jesus said no one can pluck you out of my hands. State Farm says like a good neighbor State farm is there. Jesus said I will never leave you nor will I ever forsake you. Geico says they can save you 15%. God says Hezekiah turned his face to the wall and God added unto him 15 more years. Jesus Christ is the man with the right plan. His plan gives us eternal life. (Romans 6:23) His plan give us life and life more abundantly (John 10:10)

HE CAME HERE FOR US, LEFT HERE FOR US AND IS COMING BACK FOR US

The key 🔑component to this message is who came, who left, and who is coming back. Jesus came here for us. Jesus left here for us and Jesus is coming back for us. For part 1 of this message we want to discuss he (Jesus)came here for us. Paul said this is a faithful saying and worthy of all acceptance that Christ Jesus came into this world to save sinners (US). 1Timothy 1:15. The angel declared to Joseph in a dream and told him she (Mary)shall bring forth a son and they shall call his name Jesus and he shall save his people from their sins. Matthew 1:21. Luke states that the son of mankind (Jesus) is come to seek and to save that is lost (Luke 19:10). There are manifold blessings to Jesus coming here for us. He come that we may have life and life more abundantly. He come that we above all may prosper and be in health as our soul prospers. Stay tuned tomorrow for part 2 of he came here for us, left here for us and he is coming back for us.

He Came Here For Us, Left Here For Us And Is Coming Back For Us Part 2

He came here for us, left here for us and he is coming back for us PART 2: Today we center our minds on: He left here for us. To which we can imagine it was challenging to see/hear someone that had opened blinded eyes, unstopped death *and* raised the dead leaving them. Jesus said to them let not your heart be troubled. If you believe in God believe also in me. In my father's house there are many mansions if were not so I would have told you. I go away to prepare a place for you. If I go and prepare a place for you I am coming again to receive you unto myself that where I am there you may be also and where I go you know and the way you know. Thomas said Lord we don't know where you are going and how can we know the way? Jesus said to him I am the way the truth and the life. No one comes to the father but by me. (John 14:1-6). Jesus said it was expedient (necessary) that I go away because if I don't the comforter (Paraclete) will not come. I will send you another comforter which is the Holy Ghost. Part 3 tomorrow

HE CAME HERE FOR US, LEFT HERE FOR US AND IS COMING BACK FOR US PART 4

He came here for us, left here for us and he is coming back for us part 4: Jesus gave us all the signs of what will happen and is happening before he comes back for us. Example: There will be wars and rumors of wars. Earthquakes in different places. Paul said in the last days perilous times (dangerous) shall come. EXAMPLE: People will become lovers of pleasure more than lovers of God. They will become unthankful, unholy, traitors, children will be disobedient to their parents. Many say that the Lord delays his coming. But be rest assured he is coming back. He gave the parable of the 10 virgins. 5 were wise and 5 were foolish. The 5 foolish took no oil in their lamps (The oil typifies the Holy Ghost). At midnight ⏰there was a cry made. Behold (look) the bridegroom comes go you out to meet him. The 5 wise only had enough for themselves. We don't know when he is coming but Jesus told us to be ready for no one knows the day or hour when the son of man comes. Matthew 25. Paul said I would that you sorrow not even as others which have no hope. For if we believe that Jesus died and rose again. Them them he will bring with us. For the Lord himself will descend from heaven with a shout . To be continued

MORE OF HIM & LESS OF OURSELVES EQUALS VICTORY

We can/will achieve victory in our life when we allow more of him (Jesus) and less of ourselves. Jesus said if anyone will be my disciple (follower, learner) let them deny themselves take up their cross and follow him. (Matthew 16:24). Less of ourselves means we cannot go about it like burger 🍔King 👑. Have it your way. Your ways are not his ways and your thoughts 💭are not his thoughts.(Isaiah 55:8).More of him means we allow him to be number one above all . We are to love him with all our heart, mind, soul and strength. (Luke 10:27). Perhaps you are in need of things. Jesus knows what we have need of even before we ask. (Matthew 6:8). We get victory when we have our priorities in order. Seek first the kingdom of God (His way of doing things) and his righteousness and all these things will be added unto you. (Matthew 6:33). With more of him and less of ourselves we get victory because he causes us to always triumph. (2 Corinthians 2:14).

LET'S KEEP IT MOVING; GOD HAS GREAT THINGS IN STORE FOR YOU

In order to get to what God has in store for us we need to keep it moving. We should emulate Jesus and be about our fathers business. (Luke 2:49). Jesus said I must work the works of him that has sent me while it is day the night comes when no one can work. (John 9:4). Jesus kept it moving. He said the same works I do you shall do and greater works because I go to the father. (John 14:12). We should be determined to be steadfast, unmovable, always abiding in the work of the Lord for as much as you know that your labor is not in vain. (1 Corinthians 15:58). Paul kept it moving. He said I am forgetting those things which are behind and I reach to what is before me I press toward the mark of the high calling of God which is in Christ Jesus. (Philippians 3:14). The late Martin Luther King said if you can't fly RUN, if you can't RUN, WALK, if you can't WALK CRAWL. But by all means KEEP MOVING.

Let's Keep It Moving; God Has Great Things In Store For You Part 2

PART 2: As disciples of Jesus Christ we are instructed to keep it moving. If you continue in my word you are indeed my disciples. (John 8:31). We receive what God has in store for us when we keep it moving. Jesus said abide (remain) in me and I in you can ask what you will and it shall be done. (John 15:4). Keep it moving in spite of being taken for granted. Let us not be weary in well doing for in due season we will reap if we faint not. (Galatians 6:9). To keep it moving we must not carry excess baggage 👜. Paul said let us lay aside every weight and the sin which easily beset us. Let us run 🏃the race with patience which is set before us. How do we do that? We do it by looking to Jesus the author and finisher of our faith. (Hebrews 12:2).

THE LORD CAN GET IT TO US, IF WE LET HIM GET IT THROUGH US PART 1

May we be rest assured that the Omnipotent (All powerful) God can get what is needed to us if we let (Allow) him to get it through us God want to use us He want us to be a vessel unto honor therefore he wants to purge us causing us to be sanctified and meet for the master's use. (2 Timothy 2:21). Our outward will perish while the inward is renewed day by day. (2 Corinthians 4:16).We are not the same when we let him get things through us. Therefore if anyone be in Christ they are a new creation old things are passed away and behold all things become new. (2 Corinthians 5:17).

HE WILL COME WHERE YOU LIVE & CAUSE YOU TO LIVE

There was a time in my life that I thought ● living was ♆Women☻and song. Like Paul when I was a child I thought ● as a child, spoke as a child and did childish things.(1 Corinthians 13:11). I now realize that true living is when Jesus is in our lives and in our heart. Whoever has the son (Jesus) has life whoever has not the son has not life (1 John 5:12). He desires that we live in so much he will come where we are (in our depression, in our anxiety, etc...) and cause us to live. Behold I stand at the door ▣(our hearts door ♥) and I knock if anyone will hear ☽my voice and open the door I will come in and sup (take up my abode) with them and them with me. (Revelations 3:20). The thief is the one that doesn't want us to live. The thief comes but to steal, kill and to destroy. I am come that you may have life and life more abundantly. (John 10:10). We can invite him in and he will be there. When you call me I will answer when you cry ☻I will say here I am. (Isaiah 58:9). May we ever call him. Whoever call upon the name of the Lord shall be saved. (Romans 10:13).

HE WILL COME WHERE YOU LIVE & CAUSE YOU TO LIVE PART 2

Part 2: Let us be reminded that we have life only through Jesus Christ. Whoever has the son (Jesus) has life and whoever has not the son has not life (1 John 5:12). He causes us to live when we believe on him. Whoever believe on the son has everlasting life and whoever doesn't believe doesn't have everlasting life but the wrath (Anger) of God abide on them.(John 3:36). You can have all the riches and still not be truly living. What does it profit one to gain the whole world and lose their own soul? (Mark 8:36). Ones life doesn't consist in the abundance of things they possess. We brought nothing into this world and it is certain we will carry nothing out. (Luke 12:15) (1Timothy 6:12). Job said naked I came from my mother's womb and naked I shall return (Job 1:21). May we strive to be as Paul. He said it is no longer I who live but Christ who lives in me (Galatians 2:20). He said for me to live is Christ and to die is gain. (Philippians 1:21).

BRING IT TO JESUS

The sermon topic today remind me of the song: What a friend we have in Jesus, all our sins and griefs to BEAR what a privilege it is to carry everything to God in PRAYER. Jesus is a friend that sticks closer than a brother. He said he will never leave us or forsake us he declared I will be with you always even to the end of the world. Whatever problem we have we can bring it to Jesus. He said cast (THROW) all your cares (ANXIETIES) upon him for he cares for you. When the load gets heavy and burdens are hard to bear. Jesus said come to me all who labor and are heavy laden and I will give you rest. (Matthew 11:28). Sometimes life can/ will be challenging. The psalmist said when my heart overwhelms me lead me to the rock that is higher than I. (Psalms 61:2). David would bring his situation to the Lord. He said I will lift my eyes to the hills from which comes my help my help comes from the Lord which made the heaven and earth. (Psalms 121:1) Please share this message with others for there are many that are searching for where to bring their problems. Jesus is the answer for the world TODAY, above him there is no other JESUS is the WAY.

BRING IT TO JESUS PART 2

BRING IT TO JESUS PART 2: The Lord not only wants us to bring our things (situations, circumstances) to him. He also wants us to bring ourselves to him. Paul said I beseech (urge) you brethren by the mercies of God. That you present (bring, give) your bodies as a living sacrifice holy and acceptable to God which is your reasonable service (What we should be doing) and be not conformed (like) to this world but be transformed (changed, different) by the renewing of your mind. That you may prove that which is good and the perfect will of God. (ROMANS 12:1) We bring ourselves to him for we are not our own but we are bought with a price (1 Corinthians 6:20). The end result of bringing ourselves to him is rest (Matthew 11:28). By bringing ourselves to him with the understanding he is to have the preeminent (number 1). Seek you first the Kingdom of God (His way of doing things) and his righteousness all these things will be added unto you. (Matthew 6:33). Bring it to Jesus he will BARE it Bring it to Jesus and he will SHARE it. Bring it to Jesus and he will CARRY it. If there is a need in your life. If you would only bring it to me.

DENIED, BETRAYED BUT I STAYED AND PRAYED PART 1

If in this life someone has denied you and/ or betrayed you. I come to let you know you are in good company. Jesus Christ in all points was tempted/ tested just like you and I. (Hebrews 4:15). The difference between us and Jesus is that he did it without ever sinning. He did no sin nor was any guile (deceit) found in his mouth. (1 Peter 2:22). When denied and betrayed we should have the mind of Christ. Let this mind be in you that was also in Christ Jesus. (Philippians 2:5). The scriptures teach us that the battle is not ours but belong to the Lord. We are not our own but have been bought with a price (1 Corinthians 6:19). We are to Pray when being denied. Mankind always ought to pray and not faint. (Luke 18:1). When we are betrayed we should pray Pray for them which despite fully use you (Matthew 5:44). May God bless you this season and this year of 2019.) let us pray one for another. We never know what battle and challenge in life one is enduring.

DENIED, BETRAYED BUT I STAYED AND PRAYED PART 2

Denied, Betrayed, But I Stayed and Prayed PART 2:If you want to know what to do when being DENIED/BETRAYED, then Jesus Christ is our supreme example. Peter denied him but he used Peter to preach his word and many were saved. Judas betrayed him for 30 pieces of silver (52 dollars and 80 cents). God knows that some things in life that happens to us are necessary to accomplish his will for your life. We know that all things work together for the good of them that love God and are the called according to his purpose. (Romans 8:28). Be encouraged to not be weary in well doing for in due season we will reap if we faint not. (Galatians 6:9). Be determined to fret not yourself because of evil doers nor be envious of workers of iniquity. (Psalms 37:1). The Bible says count it all Joy when you fall into diverse (different) temptations. (James 1:1). In spite of it all there is therefore no weapon formed against you shall prosper. (Isaiah 54:17)

THE SAVIOR IS PROVIDED FOR YOU & I

The Savior has been Provided for you and I PART 1: A SAVIOR is one who rescues, sets free or delivers. There is no greater SAVIOR than the Lord Jesus Christ. If you are in a current situation that you need rescuing from. God is our refuge and strength a very present help in trouble. (Psalms 46:1). Perhaps something has you bound and you need to be freed from it. You shall know the truth and the truth will make you free. (John 8:32). The Savior doesn't half step when he sets you free. Therefore who the son (Jesus) sets free they are free indeed (John 8:36). The Savior has been provided for us in many facets. His main facet was that Christ Jesus came into this world to save sinners. (1Timothy 1:15). If you are lost I stop by to say to you that the son of man (Jesus) come to seek and to save that which is lost. (Luke 19:10). It is his will/desire that all mankind be saved and come to the knowledge of the truth. (Timothy 2:4). May we all accept him as the SAVIOR that has been provided for you and I. Click on link below hit subscribe free of charge. Share with others the good news of the SAVIOR that has been provided for you and I.

THE SAVIOR IS PROVIDED FOR YOU & I PART 2

The Savior has been provided for you and I Part 2: By having the savior (Jesus) provided for us saves us from the wrath (Anger) of God. That's a blessing for it is a fearful thing to fall into the hands of the living God. (Hebrews 10:31). When one receives the Savior they receive protection. He/she that dwell in the secret place of the most high shall abide (remain)under the shadow of the Almighty. (Psalms 91:1). Protection from the enemy. When the enemy shall come in like a flood the spirit of the Lord will lift up a standard. (Isaiah 59:19). It is essential to our salvation that we receive the savior. Jesus said to Nicodemus that you must be born again (John 3:5). May these words marinate in our spirit and saturate our minds. Lord God we need you as our Savior we pray for every one that is reading 📖 this message has received or is now receiving you Jesus as Lord and savior of our lives. In Jesus Name we pray that these words are shared with the world and all across this world souls are accepting you as the savior. Lord I thank you for the life change you are doing in lives of many right now. From this day forward the life of every reader will not be the same. Some are drawing closer. Some are receiving the Holy Ghost. Some are coming out of sin and shame.

THE SAVIOR IS PROVIDED FOR YOU & I PART 3

The savior has been provided for you and I Part 3: We tend to make room for who/ what we want in life. Therefore we should make room for Who/ what we need in life. We need the Savior (Jesus) above all who/what we want/need in life. I heard Jesus say that without me you could do nothing. (John 15:5).The savior was provided for us through the Virgin Mary. The angel came to Joseph in a dream and told him she was going to bring forth a son and they would call his name Jesus for he shall save his people from their sins. (Matthew 1:21). The angels declared fear not for I bring you good tithings of great joy which shall be to all people. For born unto you this day in the city of David, a savior which is Christ the Lord. Luke 2:10-11).As we study ▭the life of the savior we find him saying to Joseph and Mary at the age of 12 that I must be about my father's business. (Luke 2:49). May we make room for the savior in our lives and in doing so let us let him have preeminence (number 1). (3 John 1:9). We may need this and we may need that (Food ●clothes ▨▨, shelter ▨. Jesus no what we have need of even before we ask. (Matthew 6:8). The savior wants us to have priorities. He said seek you first the Kingdom of God (his way of doing things) and his righteousness and all these things will be added unto you.(Matthew 6:33)

Jesus Looked Down But Not On You

In the context of this message they had bought a woman to Jesus looking down on her saying to him we caught this woman in the very act of adultery (John 8:4). While they looked down Jesus looked down on the ground but didn't look down on the woman. They bought dirt Jesus wrote in the dirt. They quoted to him what the law says that the law says stone her to death. (Deuteronomy 22:21) Jesus said to them in accordance to the law He that is without sin let him cast the first stone. They dropped their stones and we would have to do the same. For all have sinned and come short of the glory of God. (Romans 3:23). He told the woman that neither do I condemn you. Go in peace and sin no more. Jesus never looks down on us he will forgive us. I would that you sin not but if/when you sin you have an advocate (one who pleads the cause) with the father. Jesus is the propitiation (appeaser) for our sins and the sins of the world. (1John 2:2) If we confess our sins he is just to forgive us and the blood of his son Jesus will cleanse us from all unrighteousness. (1 John 2:9). Be blessed for Jesus looked down but not on you.

Come Out, Come Out Wherever You Are

By way of introduction the Lord knows where we are even when he called Adam and asked Adam where are you. God knew where he was and what he had done. (Genesis 3:9). Likewise he knows where we are. The psalmist said Lord you have searched me and known me. You know my down sitting and my uprising. If I make my bed 🛏in hell you are there. If I ascend into the heavens ☁you're there. If I take the wings of the morning dove and fly to the most utter part of the earth even there your right hand ✋will lead me. There are some areas of our lives that God is saying COME OUT COME OUT WHEREVER YOU ARE!! Please share this message and stay tuned for part 2 tomorrow. Please hit me up on YouTube and hit subscribe free of charge.

COME OUT, COME OUT WHEREVER YOU ARE PART 2

Come out come out wherever you are PART2: When one answer the call from God to come out they also in essence discover who they are in Christ Jesus. For you are a chosen generation a royal ♔priesthood a Holy nation a peculiar people that should show forth the praises of him who has called us out of darkness into his marvelous light. (1 Peter 2:9). When one comes out they understand how they are made and who made them. You are fearfully and wonderfully made. (PSALMS 139:14).We were made by him and for him. It is he (Jesus) that made us and not we ourselves we are his people and the sheep 🐑of his Pasture. (PSALMS 100:3).If we are to be used by God it is important to come out. For you are not your own but have been bought with a price (the blood of Jesus). (1 CORINTHIANS 6:20). I ask that you click on the link below hit us up on YouTube and subscribe free of charge. Thanks for sharing the Gospel with me. As we should all strive to COME OUT COME OUT WHEREVER WE ARE!!

Keep Up The God Work

I encourage the body of Christ today to keep up the God work in your life for when we keep up the God work we can/ will be found pleasing to God in so much that when ones ways please the Lord he makes even their enemies to be at peace with them. (Proverbs 16:7). The greatest example we can go by of keeping up the God work is Jesus Christ. At the age of 12 he said to Mary and Joseph that I must be about my fathers business. (Luke 2:49). He is the supreme example of pleasing God. When he was baptized in the river of Jordan God said this is my beloved son in whom I am well pleased. (Matthew 3:17). He said to you and I that if we delight ourselves also in him he will give us the desires of our heart. (Psalms 37:4). Keep up the God work and know that all things work together to the good of them that are the called according to his purpose. (Romans 8:28).

KEEP UP THE GOD WORK PART 2

Keep up the God work Part 2: Yes you read it right KEEP UP THE GOD WORK for God work is GOOD work. Perhaps you may feel not appreciated for your God work, but be encouraged to not be weary in well doing for in due season we will reap if we faint not. (Galatians 6:9). Others may not remember the God work you are doing but God will remember your God work. God is not unrighteous to forget your work and labor of love you have showed toward his people and do show toward his saints. (Hebrews 6:10). As you keep up the God work God as he was with his disciples he will be with you. Lo I am with you always even to the end of the world. (Matthew 28:20). May we all be as Jesus was and be about our fathers business (Luke 2:49). Jesus said I must work the work of him that sent me while it is day for the night come when no one can work. (John 9:4).

JESUS WANTS TO LIGHTEN YOUR HEAVY LOAD

Most of us can relate to having a heavy load. Good news is that Jesus wants to and can and will lighten our heavy load. Heavy loads can be from losing a love one and left with a broken heart ❤️‍🔥. Jesus said he is near them that have a broken heart and that he delivers them that have a contrite (repentant) spirit. When your load gets heavy and burdens are hard to bear. Jesus said come to me all who labor and are heavy laden and I will give you rest. (Matthew 11:28). Sometime the enemy brings heavy loads with one thing after another. God said when the enemy comes in like a flood the spirit of the Lord will lift up a standard. (Isaiah 59:19). May we be encouraged during our time of heavy loads. Let us not be weary in well doing for in due season we will reap if we faint not. (Galatians 6:9).

JESUS WANTS TO LIGHTEN YOUR HEAVY LOAD PART 2

Jesus wants to lighten your heavy load Part 2: From the study of the word, and from experience we can learn that God never promised us that we would go through life on flowers beds of ease. Job said mankind that is born of a woman is of few days and full of trouble. (Job 14:1). The load gets heavy because along with trouble there are also afflictions. Many are the afflictions (pain, suffering) of the righteous but God delivers them out of them all. (Psalms 34:19). In spite of the heavy loads and in spite of trouble Jesus can/will lighten your heavy load. God is our refuge and strength a very present help in trouble. (Psalms 46:1). In the midst of heavy loads we have the blessed assurance that Emmanuel is right there. His name shall be called Emmanuel which being interpreted means God with us. (Matthew 1:23). Jesus told his disciples saying lo I am with you always even to the end of the world. (Matthew 28:19,20).

I WON'T LET HIS GRACE GO TO WASTE

Our subject matter today is centered around 2 words, GRACE and WASTE. Grace is a gift from God through Jesus Christ. It is the unmerited favor toward undeserving mankind. We need not to let his GRACE (Favor, Mercy) go to WASTE. To WASTE is to squander, misspend, misuse. Paul after his conversion realized the importance of not letting his Grace go to waste. He said he persecuted the church and was the chief of sinners. But had a GRACE encounter with Jesus on Damascus road. He declared later that by the Grace of God I am what I am. He said he labored more than all but it was not himself but the Grace of God which was bestowed (gifted)upon him. He also said I do not frustrate (waste) the Grace of God. Letting them know that if the law saved them then Christ died in vain. Told the Corinthian church that if Christ did not rise then his preaching and their faith is in vain (useless). He told them that Jesus died was buried and rose again the 3rd day according to the scriptures. May we as Paul did not let his Grace go to WASTE. For none of us are saved by our works of righteousness but according to his mercy he saved us (Titus 3:5). We are saved by GRACE through FAITH, not of WORKS, not of OURSELVES, lest we should BOAST. It is the GIFT OF GOD. (EPHESIANS 2:8).

I WON'T LET HIS GRACE GO TO WASTE PART 2

I won't let his grace go to waste part 2: Grace is a free gift from God through Jesus Christ. We have not earned it nor done anything to deserve it. satan desires that we let it go to waste. But we are not ignorant concerning his devices lest he get an advantage of us. Since we cannot save ourselves we should be grateful for the grace of God. For we are saved by grace through faith not of ourselves not of works lest we boast it is the gift of God. (Ephesians 2:8). Ways in which we let it go to waste is through not understanding. Proverbs says in all your getting get understanding. We let it go to waste from lack of knowledge. He said my people perish (die) from lack of knowledge.

CHOOSE TO LOSE & BE IN IT TO WIN IT

In the context of this message we lose our life by receiving/keeping faith in Jesus Christ. Whosoever believe in him should not perish but have everlasting life. (John 3:16). The way to lose our life is to become/be a disciple (a learner and follower) of Christ. If anyone will be my disciple let them deny themselves take up their cross and follow me. (Matthew 16:24). When we are in it to win it we should be like Paul who said I count them but dung (Rubbish) that I might win Christ. (Philippians 3:8). Joshua said: Choose you this day who you will serve, as for me and my house we will serve the Lord. (Joshua 24:15). Moses the Law giver said: I set before you death and life, blessings and curses. Then he said choose life. (Deuteronomy 30:19). May we choose to lose our life that we may save it. We choose to lose and we avoid being separated from God. For the wages of sin is death but the gift of God is eternal life. (Romans 6:23).

CHOOSE TO LOSE & BE IN IT TO WIN IT PART 2

Choose to lose & be in it to win it .PART 2 : In order to save our life we must lose our life. How so? you may ask. We lose our way of thinking ☺how to go about obtaining victory and we seek after Christ way of obtaining victory. Let this mind be in you that was also in Christ Jesus. You may have great intellect and a good EDUMACATION and do it the way you feel is the right way. The book 📖of Proverbs says there is a way that seems right to a person, but the end are the ways of death. We must understand that Jesus said I am the way the truth and the life, no one comes to the father but by me. We should be in it to win it therefore we should serve him (Jesus) and him only should we serve. When we are in it to win it Jesus causes us to always triumph. When we are in it to win it no weapon formed against you shall prosper (Isaiah 54:17). When we are in it to win it. Jesus said upon this rock will I build my church and the gates of hell shall not prevail against it. May we all be steadfast unmovable, always abiding in the work of the Lord for as much as you know that your labor is not in vain.

THE LORD DESIRES TO DO AN INSIDE JOB ON US PART 2

Part 2: When the Lord is doing an inside job on us it is important that we do as the Bible says: Lean not to your own understanding but trust in the Lord, in all your ways acknowledge him and he will direct your path. (Proverbs 3:5) When the Lord does an inside job we don't treat him like we are at burger 🍔king 👑. We are not going to have it our way. My thoughts 💭are not your thoughts. Neither my ways your ways says the Lord. (Isaiah 55:8). The devil may be on your track trying to turn you back. That is why we should submit (obey)to God resist the devil and he will flee from us. (James 4:7). Be encouraged to do as Paul. He said I press toward the mark for the prize of the high calling of God in Christ Jesus (Philippians 3:14). He told us to be confident of this very thing that he which has began a good work in us will perform it until the day of Jesus Christ (Philippians 1:6).

DID YOU GET THE TEXT THAT I SENT YOU?

Many of us are familiar with sending/receiving a text. The text in reference today does not derive from being with Verizon, A T@T, nor Sprint but from the Bible (BASIC INSTRUCTIONS BEFORE LEAVING EARTH). The most important text is sent from God. Many of our young people text in shorthand. I am going to give shorthand texting today and relate it from natural to spiritual. Natural there is a text BAE (before anyone else) We need a BAE Spiritually but not meaning before anyone else. For the Lord said we shall have no other god before him. We need a Spiritual BAE (BORN AGAIN EXPERIENCE) Jesus told Nicodemus that you must be born again. We need to get the same text. Another natural text is LOL (LAUGH OUT LOUD). We need a spiritual LOL (LIVE OUT LOUD) Let your light so shine that mankind may see your good works and glorify our father which is in heaven is how we LOL (LIVE OUT LOUD). Another natural text is SMH (SHAKE MY HEAD) Spiritual we need a SMH (SALVATION MEANS HEAVEN) We get salvation that means we get heaven. Therefore we need to get the text. John 10: Jesus said I am the door of the sheep and my me if anyone enters they shall be saved. John14:6 Jesus said I am the way the truth and the life. Acts 4:12 Neither is their salvation in any other for there is no other name under heaven given unto men that whereby we must be saved.

DID YOU GET THE TEXT
THAT I SENT YOU? PART 2

PART 2: Did you get the text that I sent you? The best and most important text we can receive comes from the word of God. We need the text to have faith. Faith comes by hearing and hearing by the word of God. (Romans 10:17). The text is not from readers digest or sports illustrated. All scripture is given by the inspiration of God and is profitable (beneficial) for doctrine (teaching) for reproof, for correction, for instruction (training) in righteousness (2 Timothy 3:16. The text is no fairytale but Holy men spoke as they were moved by the Holy Ghost. (2Peter 1:21). Like a baby need milk 🥛, We should desire the sincere milk of the word that we may grow thereby. As we are on this tedious (tiresome) journey. The text (word) becomes a lamp to our feet 👣and a light 💡to our pathway. May we all get the text that God is sending to us on a daily basis.

YOU MAY HAVE TO SHAKE IT; BUT IF YOU CAN TAKE IT, YOU CAN MAKE IT

There comes times in our lives that we have to shake some things off in order to make it. When Paul was bitten on the hand ✋by a viper 🐍he shook it off. Life will bite us like a viper 🐍. When life bites us we shake it off by being like a tree 🌲planted by the rivers of water 🌊we shall not be moved. Moses said stand still and see the salvation (deliverance) of the Lord. Jesus said in the world 🌍we will have tribulations but if we can take it we can make it. In the midst of tribulations he said be of good cheer for I have overcome the world. We will face temptation but if we can take it we can make it. There is no temptation that has overtaken you but such as common to mankind God with the temptation will make a way of escape so that you are able to bear it. Shake it off and count it all Joy when you fall into diverse (different) temptations. Knowing that the trying of your faith works patience. If you can take it you can make it. Life is seemingly unfair and your kindness is taken for weakness. Be encouraged to not be weary in well doing for in due season we will reap if we faint not. May we be determined to shake it off for if we can take it we can make it.

NO DEAL SATAN, WE MUST LIVE BY HIS EVERY WORD

Jesus Christ is our supreme example of not making a deal with satan. When satan (the tempter) said to him turn these stones into bread 🍞Jesus made no deal 🗡with him but told him it is written that mankind shall not live by bread alone but by every word 📖which proceeds out of the mouth 🪶of God. When satan said to Jesus to throw himself down Jesus told him what was written: that we should not tempt the Lord thy God. When satan tried to offer him the kingdoms of the world 🌍if he would bow down and worship him. Jesus told him to get the hence for thou shall worship the Lord thy God and him only shall I serve. We are to take the same mindset (Let this mind be in you that was also in Christ Jesus) and make no deal with satan. We should give no place to the devil. We are to submit ourselves (obey) to God, resist the devil and he will flee from us. We are not to be ignorant (not knowing) to his devices. The devil is our adversary (the arch enemy of God) he is seeking who he may devour. No deal satan I must live by his every word.

You May Be Under Attack; But If You Are Under The Blood, You Are Right On Track

There are times in our life when we are under attack (subjected to the enemy, vulnerable)the key ✒thing is to be covered under the blood of Jesus. The blood is precious (VALUABLE) Grandma said what can wash away my sin? Nothing but the blood. What can make me whole again? Nothing but the. The blood has power. Grandma said again it reaches the highest mountain it flow and it will never lose its power. The blood is significant (essential,important) Without the shedding of blood there is no remission (no removal) of our sins. We were purchased by the blood. For we were not redeemed by corruptible things (things that are going to pass away) such as silver and gold, but by the precious blood of the lamb (Jesus Christ). The blood protects us when we are under attack. When the enemy comes in like a flood the spirit of the Lord will lift up a standard against it. When under the blood you are right on track for no weapon formed against you shall prosper (Isaiah 54:17). When under the blood you dwell in the secret place of the most high and abide (remain) under the shadow of the almighty (Psalms 91). May we know that when under attack and under the blood we are right on track.

WHERE ARE YOU?

God sometimes ask questions he already know the answer to. Adam heard his voice walking in the cool of the day and God said Adam where are you? Perhaps God ask questions he already knows the answer to in order to get our attention as to where we are in certain areas of our lives. Adam was in an area of disobedience. Where are you/we in areas of our life? Since God is Love we should examine where are we in our love. God commands us to Love him with all our heart all our mind and with all our soul. We are to love our neighbor as ourself. Paul said though I speak with tongues of angels and men and don't have love I am nothing. He said I am a tinkling cymbal or a sounding brass (just making noise). Where are you? How can we say we love God who we have not seen and hate our brother/sister who we see daily? Where are you/we? Love is a key area where we should analyze where are we at? This is part 1 but an integral part as to WHERE ARE YOU?

WHERE ARE YOU? PART 2

Part 2: In part 1 of where are you? We discussed the area of love. Love is an area every child of God should relate to in their daily lives. Even faith works by Love. Faith, hope, Love and the greatest of these 3 is Love. Today we want to look 👀at where are we in the area of our faith. How is faith obtained? Faith comes by hearing and hearing by the word of God. Is faith important? Yes because without faith it is impossible to please God. Anyone who comes to God must believe that he is and that he is a rewarder of them which diligently seek him. You may say I don't have a whole lot of faith. You don't have to have a whole LOT just use the little you GOT. If you have faith the size of a mustard seed you can speak to mountains (situations, circumstances) tell mountains to move and go yonder place. Doubt not in your heart but believe those things you say shall come to pass you shall have whatever you say. I pray we be where we need to be in the area of LOVE and FAITH.

WHERE ARE YOU? PART 3

Part 3: Let us be ever mindful that God know where we are. He know our down sitting and our uprising. The psalmist said if I ascend into the heavens (clouds ⌒) he is there. If I make my bed 🛏in hell he is there. His eyes 👀are in every place looking at the evil and the good. Today we want to ask where are you in the area of WORSHIP and PRAISE? Jesus told the woman at the well: That God is a spirit and seek such to WORSHIP him. They that WORSHIP him MUST WORSHIP him in spirit and in truth . Where are you? For he also said we should WORSHIP the Lord our God and him only should we serve. May we WORSHIP in having adoration for him. Where are you? May we not be ashamed to WORSHIP him. Where are you? For if we be ashamed to own him before mankind he said he will be ashamed to own us before his father.

WHERE ARE YOU? PART 4

Part 4: Today we ask WHERE ARE YOU in the area of PRAISE? One characteristic of every child of God should be that we give God the PRAISE. PRAISE is comely for the upright (It's becoming of us to PRAISE GOD). Psalm 150 tells us ways to PRAISE him (cymbals, stringed instruments, trumpet, organ, dance 🎵). Where are you? For he also said let everything/everyone that have breath PRAISE the Lord. We should PRAISE him in spite of hardships or circumstances. David said I will bless the Lord at all times and his praise shall continually be in my mouth. If we are going to brag of anything it should be about the goodness of the Lord. David said my soul shall make her boast in the Lord. The humble shall hear thereof and be glad. David wanted others to praise God to he wasn't selfish. He said O magnify the Lord with me let's exalt his name together.

GOD IS AT YOUR HOUSE
AND HE IS CALLING YOU

When God is at our house it is always in our best interest. Unlike the thief that shows up at our house to steal to kill and destroy. When Jesus comes to our house he come that we may have life and life more abundantly. When he call we should answer. Today if you will hear ℋhis voice, harden not your heart behold today is the day of salvation and now is the accepted time. Jesus is saying to someone today as he said to the church ⌂at Laodicea: Behold I stand at the door 🚪(our hearts door) and knock, if anyone will hear his voice and open the door I will come in and sup (take up my abode) with them and they with me. God is at our house and we should show forth the praises of him who has called us out of darkness into this marvelous light. He has called us with an Holy calling (To set us apart) Whosoever will let them come. Thank God for his love that he is willing to come to all our house and may we all answer his call. Stay tuned tomorrow for part 2 of God is at your house and he is calling you.

DO YOU BELIEVE WE CAN DO THIS?

When we desire God to do something for us it is essential that we believe (have faith) he can do it. How is faith obtained? Faith comes by hearing 👂 ,hearing comes by the word 📖of God. Faith is important to have because without faith it is impossible to please him. When one comes to God they must believe that he is and that he is a rewarder of them that diligently seek him. You may say I don't have a lot of faith. You don't have to have a whole LOT just use the little you GOT. If you have the faith as a grain of mustard seed you can speak to mountains (situations, circumstances, etc.) Tell mountains to move and go yonder place. Doubt not in your heart but believe those things you say shall come to pass you will have whatever you say. To believe we can do this we should not go on what it look 👀like for we walk by faith and not by sight. Let us also understand that just saying I believe or have faith is not enough for faith without works is dead. And works without faith is dead also. Paul said show me your faith without your work and I will show you my faith by my works.

LET US BE THE CHANGE THAT WE WANT TO SEE IN OTHERS

While we may not can make others change. We can be the change that we want to see in others. We can let our light ♀so shine before mankind that they may see our our good works and glorify our father who is in heaven. We can be the change we want to see in others when we do as Jesus said: As I have loved you, love you one another. We can be the change we want to see in others when we love our enemies, pray for them which despite fully use us We bless them that curse us and love them that hate us. I know that may not be the norm but it is the change that Jesus want to see in others. We as Christians should strive to be the change we want to see in others. (Christian means Christlike). 2nd Corinthians 5:17 says: Therefore if anyone be in Christ they are a new creation old things are passed away and behold all things are become new. Let us be the change that we want to see in others.

WHEN YOU ARE AT YOUR LOWEST, LOOK TO THE HIGHEST

Most of us if not all of us have experienced some low points (Loss of Love one, sickness, financial, etc.) in our lives. If not grand momma says just keep living. Be encouraged when you are at your lowest to look 👀to the highest (Jesus Christ). David said when my heart overwhelm me lead me to the rock that is higher than I. That rock is Jesus when you are at your lowest he is a rock in a weary land. When you are in a storm ⛅in your life and at your lowest look to the highest for he is a shelter in the time of a storm. You may be at your lowest and doing your best to come up. Let us not be weary in well doing for in due season we will reap if we faint not. You perhaps are at your lowest and feel you can't take much more but look to the highest for he gives power to the faint (tired, weak) and to them which have no might he increases strength. Please share with others for there is many across this world 🌍that feel they are at their lowest. May we all look to the highest from where our help comes.

I FOUND THE ANSWER,
I LEARNED TO PRAY

Prayer is the sincere utterance to God by faith. We should always pray and not faint. We should pray without ceasing (Always have a prayerful mind). James said when we are afflicted we should pray. He said that the effectual prayers of a righteous person avails much. When we pray we should believe and we shall receive. Hanna prayed to have a child she believed and she received. They held a prayer meeting for Peter to be released from jail. They believed and they received. Paul and Silas prayed and song while locked in jail they believed and they received. Since God has no respect of persons, we too can pray to God for he hears and answer prayer. I found the answer when I learned to PRAY with faith to guide me along the WAY. The SON (Jesus Christ) is shining on me each DAY I found the answer I learned to PRAY 🙏

Let The Power Of The Holy Ghost Fall In This House Part 3

Part 3: When the 120 were filled with the Holy Ghost on the day of Pentecost some say they were drunk ☺and full of new wine 🍷. But they wondered how because it was only the 3rd hour of the day (9:00 A.M.) Peter stood up and said these are not drunk as you suppose, but this is that which was spoken by the Prophet Joel: In the last days says God that I will pour out of my spirit upon all flesh your sons and daughters shall prophesy old men will dream dreams and young men will see visions (Joel 2:28)(Acts 2:16-17). The Holy Ghost is here right now desiring to dwell within our temples. Stay tuned for part 4 of this series tomorrow. May we all let the power of the Holy Ghost have his way in our house 🏠, in our churches ⛪, we that are filled have within us to change the world 🌍 . (The world system)

LET THE POWER OF THE HOLY GHOST FALL IN THIS HOUSE PART 4

Part 4: while Jesus was still here he told his disciples that it was expedient (necessary) that I go away, if I don't go away the comforter (Paraclete) will not come. I am going to send you another comforter which is the Holy Ghost he will lead you and guide you into all truth (The truth will make us free) He will bring all things to our remembrance what I have told you. Therefore we can see the importance of having the power of the Holy Ghost. God used them after they were filled with his power in Acts 2 they broke bread from house to house (Fellowship). They shared their goods (Love). Those that were not filled saw the power of God in others and were pricked (convicted)in their heart and said men and brethren what must we do to be saved? Peter said REPENT (become Godly sorry) Every one of you and be baptized in the name Lord Jesus Christ and you shall receive the gift of the Holy Ghost

LET THE POWER OF THE HOLY GHOST FALL IN THIS HOUSE PART 5

Part5: The KEY 🔑word to receiving or having the power of God falling in our house (Our bodies are the temple of the Holy Ghost) is LET (which means allow). If we LET(Allow) the Holy Ghost do/be what he want to do/be the Holy Ghost has no issues with coming in Jesus said I will be in you a well of water springing up into everlasting life. He said to the church at Laodicea Behold I stand at the door 🚪and I knock if anyone will 👂my voice and open the door (our hearts door) I will come in and sup (take up my abode) with them and them with me. REVELATIONS 3:20. While Peter was preaching the Holy Ghost fell upon the Gentile (non-Jews) They received the Holy Ghost and were baptized in the name (Character, and authority) of the Lord Jesus. The power of the Holy Ghost is readily available to all mankind. The promise is to you, your children, and all that are afar off even as many as the Lord shall call.

Jesus Paid It All & Let Us Keep The Change

It has been well said that we owed a debt (sin debt) we could not pay. Jesus paid a debt (our sin debt) he did not owe. He desires to redeem mankind not with corruptible things (things that will pass away with the using there of) like silver and gold but with his precious blood. He paid it all with his blood which is very significant. Without the shedding of blood there is no remission of our sins. Not only did he pay it all but he let us keep the change. The change of a new life is what we can keep. Therefore if anyone be in Christ he is a new creation old things are passed away and behold all things are become new. May we be grateful for the fact that Jesus paid it all and all to him we owe our sins were crimson stained but he will make it white as snow ✳.

LETS FAITH IT, TILL WE MAKE IT

Some say let's FAKE IT (Pretend) till we MAKE IT. I say today let's FAITH IT (trust, believe) till we MAKE IT. How do we obtain faith? Faith comes by hearing �֎and hearing by the word ▢of God. You may say I don't have a whole lot of faith. You don't have to have a whole LOT just use the little you GOT. If you have the faith as a grain of mustard seed you can speak to mountains ⌂and tell them to move and go yonder place. Doubt not in your heart but believe those things which you say shall come to pass you shall have whatever you say. Let's faith it till we make it even if we can't see it. For we walk by faith and not by sight. If we are to make it, then having faith is essential. For without faith it is impossible to please him. Please share and refresh others for those who refresh shall themselves be refreshed.

I WANT MY DADDY'S
BLESSING BACK

I give praise to God from whom all blessings flow. Every good and perfect gift comes from above. The devil aim is to take or cause us to not receive the blessings of God. The thief comes but to steal, kill and destroy. I want my daddy's blessings back for he come that we might have life and life more abundantly. Daddy Jesus want us to have our blessings back for he would that we prosper and be in health even as our soul prospers. No reason why we can't have our daddy's blessings back if we delight (do that which bring pleasure to God) ourselves in him he will give us the desires of our heart. Be encouraged to know that eye ◉ has not seen nor ear 👂heard neither has it entered into the heart ♥of mankind what the Lord has prepared for them that love him. I want my daddy's blessings back for he shall supply all our needs according to his riches in glory by Christ Jesus. He will open the windows of heaven and pour out blessings that there is not room to receive. Please share and REFRESH others for they that REFRESH shall themselves be REFRESHED

TEAMWORK WILL WORK

No wonder the psalmist says: O how good and pleasant it is for brethren to dwell together in unity. Teamwork will work because Iron sharpens Iron. Sheep 🐑begat sheep 🐑and begat Love. It works because 2 are better than 1 and a 3 fold cord is not quickly broken. Teamwork worked with Paul and Silas (they prayed 🎵and song praises to God. Teamwork worked in a fiery furnace (They said the God we serve is able) Teamwork worked on the day of Pentecost (They were all filled with the Holy Ghost).

HAVE YOU HEARD?

What the Lord has said about us far outweighs what others have said. He said that we are more than a conqueror through him that love us. He said when the enemy comes in like a flood, the spirit of the Lord will lift up a standard. I heard him say about you that Greater is he that is within you than he that is within the world. He said about you that no weapon formed against you would prosper. I heard him say if trust him will with all our heart he will direct our path. He said this about you, delight yourself (do that which brings pleasure to God) also in him he will direct your path. He has abide (remain)in him and his word in you that you can ask what you will and it shall be done. He said about you and I that they that wait upon the Lord he will renew their strength. He shall mount upon you as wings of an eagle you shall run and not get weary, walk and not faint.

It's Coming Just Stay The Course

Praise the Lord, from whom blessings flow. There are things we desire to come to us (Problems solved, Situations resolved, circumstances beyond our control, etc.) Life gets hard even for the child of God. I say to you to endure hardness as a good soldier of Jesus Christ. It's coming in spite of having to stand a lot (sometimes seemingly all alone, going through one thing after another, etc....). Be encouraged having done all to stand, stand therefore!! As you stay the course, continue to lift your eyes 👀to the hills from where your help come (From the Lord). In order to stay the course we should lay aside every weight and the sin which easily beset us (Throw us off course, hinders / stop the will of God for our lives) and let us run 🏃the race with patience that is set before us. Perhaps you may say how in the world 🌍can I do that? By looking to Jesus, the author (He is the first and the last) and finisher (Alpha and Omega) (The beginning and the end) of our faith.

God's Recipe For Survival

On the natural side of life we love good RECIPES (EXAMPLE: COLONEL SANDERS KFC, MRS. Smiths Pies, Grandmothers home made banana pudding) Likewise there is nothing better than God's RECIPE for SURVIVAL. For every temptation God's recipe for survival (there is a way of escape) For every sickness (By his stripes you are healed). What the devil means for evil, you can survive he is seeking whom he may devour, but I heard the Lord say cast (throw) all your cares upon him for he cares for you. The load may be heavy and burdens are hard to bear. Jesus said come to me all who labor and are heavy laden, I will give you rest.

FOR THE RIGHT HOOKUP YOU ONLY HAVE TO LOOK UP

I am familiar with a hookup on both sides of life (natural and spiritual) There are some on the natural I forever REGRET, there are some on the spiritual that I will never FORGET. What we all need is not just a hookup but the RIGHT hookup. David found the right hookup when he lift his eyes 👀to the hills from which his help come from (Our help comes from the Lord). Moses declared that the people could look up at the brazen serpent and live. Jesus declared that as Moses lifted up the brazen serpent in the wilderness. Even so the son of man (Jesus) be lifted. He is the right hookup for all we need. Jesus said if I be lifted from the earth 🌍then will I draw all men/ mankind unto me.

Whatever is Lying At Your Door, Let's Lay It Aside And Let Him In

The lesson text today is the story of Cain and Abel. God told Cain if you do well will you not be accepted? But if not then sin lies (is crouching) at your door 🚪. We should lay aside anything that hinder us (lifestyle, habits, self, flesh, devil, etc.) Paul says let us lay aside every WEIGHT and SIN which

easily beset us. All WEIGHTS are not SINS, but all SINS are WEIGHTS. Whatever it is that causes us to stumble or be a stumble let's lay it aside and let Jesus in. John said I decrease (less of me) he must increase (more of him) Jesus prayed not my will God but let your will be done. I am still learning that our ways are not God ways and our thoughts are not his thoughts. No matter how seemingly it seems to be right. There is a way which seems right to mankind but the end are the ways of death. (a seem right way can lead to death). For the wages of sin is death (separation from God) but the gift of God is eternal life.

A Truly Rewarding Life, Is A Life We All Need

We as a whole desire a REWARDING LIFE (Health, Happiness, Success, Etc.) A truly REWARDING LIFE (A Life with Jesus) is a LIFE we all need. A life where he would that we prosper and be in health, as our soul prospers. A life that by denying ourselves we can have all that pertains to life and Godliness and in the world to come everlasting life. With Jesus as author and finisher of our faith we shall have life and life more abundantly. Peace that surpasses all understanding. Joy unspeakable and full of Glory.

HE IS THE DOOR THAT I ADORE

Jesus Christ said: I am the door ▦(access way)of the sheep 🐑(we are the sheep of his Pasture). By me if anyone enters he shall be saved. We should love him with all our heart, mind 🐑soul and strength. Above all we should adore him for all things work together to the good of them that love God and are the called according to his purpose. Great things are in store for you when you adore him. For eye 👁has not seen nor ear 👂has heard neither has it entered into the heart of mankind what the Lord has prepared for them that love him. I pray that that Jesus Christ be the door ▦we all adore. Worthy is the lamb which was slain before the foundation of the world.

THE BENEFITS AND RESULTS
OF WALKING WITH GOD

From experience and study ▢of God word we will see the benefits (an advantage or profit from something) and the results (effect or outcome of something) of walking ▲with God. Jesus is our supreme example. When John baptized him God said this is my beloved son in whom I am well pleased. When our ways (our walk with God) please the Lord he will make even our enemies to be at peace with us. The benefits and results of walking with God is a new life. Therefore if anyone be in Christ he is a new creation, old things (lifestyle, stress, etc.) are passed away, behold all things are become new (Joy, Peace, Everlasting life) We will experience the benefits of walking with God if we delight ourselves (do that which pleases God) also in him and he will give us the desires of your heart May God bless you.

Exposure To The Son Will Prevent Us From Burning, While At The Same Time Keep Us Burning Part 1

Our lesson text today is centered around the word EXPOSURE (coming in contact with someone or something). While on the natural side of life EXPOSURE to the sun ☀️will cause you to burn. EXPOSURE to the SON (Jesus)will keep you from burning. EXPOSURE to the son will prevent us from burning in hell (a place of a burning furnace of fire 🔥: there will be wailing 😫and gnashing of teeth. Exposure to the son will prevent us from burning from the lust of the flesh the lust of the eyes 👀 and from the pride of life. We all should get more Exposure to the Son. Therefore we should draw near to God and he will draw near to us. You May say how can I when satan is on my TRACK trying to turn me BACK? We do it by submitting (being obedient) ourselves to God, resist the devil and he will flee (Runaway)from you. Thanks everyone I am honored and appreciative of all that tune in to broadcast and listen and read .My desire is to build up the Kingdom of God.

EXPOSURE TO THE SON WILL PREVENT US FROM BURNING, WHILE AT THE SAME TIME KEEP US BURNING PART 2

Exposure to the Sun ☀ will cause you to burn on the natural side of life. Yet exposure to the SON (Jesus Christ) will prevent you from burning. It is his will that none should perish (Burn in Hell). But that all come to repentance (Burn with fire 🔥 of the Holy Ghost).

GET BEHIND ME DEVIL, I AM GOING TO ANOTHER LEVEL

The devil tried Jesus so certainly he is going to try us. He said to Jesus if you be the son of God, turn these stones into bread. Jesus told him that man shall not live by bread alone but by every word that proceeds (comes forth) out of its mouth. We are to submit (be subject to) ourselves to God, resist (withstand, oppose) the devil and he will flee (run away) from you. We are to be sober (serious minded) be vigilant (alert, observant) because your adversary the devil (the arch enemy of God) walks about as a roaring lion seeking who he may devour. We can all go to another level by following the example of Jesus said I must be about my father's business. Also the example of Paul who said I am forgetting those things which are behind and reaching forth to those things which are before me. I press toward the mark of the high calling of God which is in Christ Jesus.

COME GET THE LOVE HE HAS PROMISED YOU

God desires that we receive the greatest love that there is. For greater love has no one than this. Than a man would lay down his life for his friend. His love is AGAPE love (Unconditional). He loves us to the point he gave us his best. For God so loved the world, that he gave his only begotten son that whosoever believe (trust, rely upon) in him should not perish but have everlasting life. What great love he has for us in that while we were yet sinners he loved us. Let's not be like the church in revelation that left their first love. We love him not because we are so deserving or worthy are were so righteous. We love him because he first loved us. If you feel unloved because of these times (a time when the Love of many will wax cold. Come get the love he has promised you. May the love of God rest, rule, abide with us henceforth now and forever amen 🙏.

PUT YOUR WAIT ON IT

To receive an expected end (future, hope, success) We must put our WAIT on it. Not our physical WEIGHT, but WAIT as in being patient. It is with patience we possess our soul. When you have done what he told you to do, you must put your wait on it. For after you have done the will of God you have need of patience that you might receive the promise. We put our wait on it by letting patience have its perfect work. Grandma 😊 said it like this you can't hurry God you just have to WAIT, put your trust in him no matter how long it TAKES. He is a God you can't HURRY he will be there don't you WORRY. He may not come when you want him but he will be there right on time. Put your wait on it. For they that wait on the Lord he shall renew their strength, he will mount up on you like wings of an eagle 🦅you shall run 🏃and not get weary you shall walk and not faint. God bless you may we all put our wait on it it and receive the perfect will of God.

JESUS IS THE WAY

Jesus is the answer for the world 🌍TODAY, above him there's no other Jesus is the WAY. He is the way to eternal life for the gift (Jesus)of God is eternal life. He is the way to the father, he said to Thomas I am the way the truth and the life no man comes to the father but by me. Jesus declared that I am the door (access way) of the sheep (we are the sheep of his Pasture) by me (Jesus) if anyone enters they shall be saved. Jesus is the way of salvation for neither is there salvation in any other for there is no other name under heaven given unto men whereby we must be saved. He is the way of safety for the name of the Lord is a strong tower and the righteous run 🏃into it and they are safe. May we be encouraged to look to him from which comes our help. May we come to him when we labor (tired, frustrated) and heavy laden and he will give us rest. God bless you with great honor and appreciation I am that you tune into hear 👂and see these messages and share with others I am grateful for all of you 💕

WHAT ARE WE GOING TO DO WITH THIS MAN PART 1

We like Pilate had to or will have to do something with our Lord and savior Jesus Christ. His desire is that all mankind be saved and come to the knowledge of the truth. When I was lost he came to seek and save that which is lost. What are we to do when we are thirsty? He said if anyone thirst let him come after me, believe on me as the scripture 📖has said and out of your belly (your innermost) shall flow rivers of living water. What are we going to do with him when the load gets heavy? He said come to me all that labor and are heavy laden and I will give you rest. What are we going to do with him when we need direction? He said lean not to your own understanding, but trust (rely upon, have faith) in the Lord, in all your ways acknowledge him and he will direct your path. I ask that you help me to share this part 1 of What are we going to do with this man with others God bless you amen 🙏.

WHAT ARE WE GOING TO DO WITH THIS MAN PART 4

When given a choice of what to do with this man (Jesus) the people said away with this man(Jesus) and give us Barrabus (A murderer) concerning Jesus they said crucify him crucify him. What they did with him had a great effect on us. Jesus declared that if I be lifted (on the cross) from the earth then will I draw all men unto me. He said to them destroy this body and in 3 days I will raise it up again. He was speaking concerning his death. When he allowed them (no man took his life he laid (willingly) it down for himself. I come to learn that voluntarily (willingly) or involuntarily (unwittingly) we all are going to to something with this man. For God has highly exalted him and given him a name above every name that at the name of Jesus every knee shall bow 🙇and every tongue 👅shall confess that he is Lord. Lord Jesus I bow 🙇now and I confess now that you are Lord. I am thankful for this 4 part series. I would like for you to click on link below and share with others. God bless you 🙏

WHAT IS THAT MAN DOING AT YOUR HOUSE? PART 1

We are not referring to the man that come to fix your sink, but the man that come to fix your heart (Jesus).When Jesus is at our house, he stands at the door ▤and knock, saying If anyone will hear 𝒟my voice and open the door ▤I will come in and sup (take up my abode) with him and him/ mankind with me. The question in reality is what are we allowing him to do at our house? When we let him do what he desires he will be in us a well of water ❀springing up into everlasting life. May he be at/ in all our house, causing us all to be about our father's business.

I COME THIS FAR, FIND NO FAULT, I FEEL LIKE GOING ON

We may find fault in (life, things, people, ourselves). Yet there is one in which I find no fault. That is the immaculate (faultless, I unstained) One Jesus Christ, He (Jesus) knew no sin nor was any guile (no deceit) found in his mouth. It is impossible for him to lie. He is not a man that he should lie nor the son of man that he should repent. He does not change. Jesus Christ the same yesterday today and forever. I find no fault in him he promised to never leave us or forsake us. I find no fault in him he is the perfect sacrifice (the lamb of God who takes away the sin of the world 🌍).

GRACE TO FACE THE RACE PART 1

Jesus said in the world we will have tribulations, but be of good cheer for he has overcome the world. Be encouraged to know that he gives Grace (God's unmerited favor) to face the race. Paul went to him 3 times asking for a thorn in the flesh to depart. The Lord said to him my Grace is sufficient (There is enough Grace to get us through) in the time of weakness his strength is made perfect. We are not saved of our own merits. For by Grace are you saved through faith, not of works, not of yourselves, unless we should boast, it is the gift of God. If we keep the faith we can having done all to stand, we can stand therefore.

IT IS THROUGH JESUS THAT WE MAKE IT PART 1

We make it through Jesus no matter the circumstance, or how overwhelming life gets. With him all things are possible. We made it thus far through Jesus. If it had not been the Lord who was on our side, when men (The enemy) rose against us they would have swallowed (drowned us in fear, life's troubles, etc.) us up. When the devil says you can't. Let's be like Paul and say I can do all things through Christ which strengthens me. We are counted as sheep for the slaughter, but we are more than a conqueror through him that love us. We make it through him because he said upon this rock, I will build my church and the gates of hell shall not prevail against. Through him we win. He causes us to always triumph. We are safe through him. The name of the Lord is a strong tower, the RIGHTEOUS, runs into it and they are safe.

HOW MAY I HELP YOU?

These words we see on the back of employees at Walmart (How May I help you?) The lord will help us with things that Walmart doesn't stock (Burdens, Trials, etc). Therefore we can lift our eyes 👀to the hills from where our help comes. We can look 👀to Jesus the author and finisher of our faith. When in need of help we can cast all our care upon him for he cares for us. When your load gets heavy and burdens are hard to bear, Jesus said come to me all who labor and are heavy laden and I will give you rest. He says prove me (Try me) and see if I will open the window of heaven and pour you out blessings that you will not have room to receive.

HOW MAY I HELP YOU? PART 2

PART 2: The Lord is there to help you just as he did the Bible patriarchs that we read about. There is no respect of persons with God. (Romans 2:11). If Abraham was here he would tell us that he will help you with what seems no way. When God told him he was going to father a child in his old age he laughed 😄. When God helped him produce the promised seed. He said is there anything too hard for God. (Genesis 18:14). If he helped Abraham he will and has helped us. You may have a heavy load and burdens are hard to bear. The Lord hear your cry for help. He says when you call me I will answer, when you cry I will say here I am. (Isaiah 58:9). Help is available Jesus said come to me all who labor and are heavy laden and I will give you rest. (Matthew 11:28). Help is on the way. He said ask and it shall be given, seek and you will find, knock 👊and the door 🚪shall be opened unto you. (Matthew 7:7). God is well able to help you. He can do exceedingly, abundantly above all that you think, according to the power that works in us. (Ephesians 3:20).

Jesus Paid It All Part 2

It has been well said that Jesus paid it all, and all to him I OWE, my sin was crimson stain, he washed them white as SNOW ❄. He paid it all not with corruptible things (things that will pass away with the using thereof) such as silver and gold from our vain traditions, but by the previous blood of the lamb (the blood of Jesus) because he paid it all we can eat the good of the land. He paid it all therefore we can overcome by the blood and testimonies.

THE LORD IS THE STRENGTH OF MY LIFE AND THE SOURCE OF MY STRENGTH

When we are in need of strength Jesus should be our source. Jesus himself said to his disciples: Without me you could do nothing. When building on the wall Nehemiah had the right source. He said the Joy of the Lord is our strength. Apostle Paul had the Lord as the source of his strength and he declared that I can do all things through Christ which strengthens me. David a man after God's own heart had the Lord as the source of his strength. David said the Lord is my light and my salvation whom shall I fear? The Lord is the strength of my life of whom shall I be afraid? When the wicked even my enemies and my foes came up against me they stumbled and fell. God was with all of these Bible patriarchs and he will be with us when we allow him to be the source of our strength.

GOD WILL STRAIGHTEN US OUT

On last week we talked about God will straighten it out. Today we want to focus on God will straighten us out. We are straightened out through Jesus Christ and his word. Jesus said we are clean through the word which he has spoken to us. David knew the importance of being straightened out through his word. He declared your word Oh Lord have I hid in my heart that I might not sin against you. He said a young man is cleansed by taking heed to his word. After being Straightened out the word became to him a lamp to his feet and a light to his pathway. When God word straightened him out he realized that a good man steps are ordered by the Lord and the Lord delights (have pleasure) in his ways. God straightened David out and he can/will straighten us out. May we all allow God to straighten us out that we may let our light shine before men that they may see our good works and glorify our father in heaven.

PRAISE HIM IN SPITE OF AND NOT BECAUSE OF

Praise the Lord everyone!! Thou we are tried by fire. (1 Corinthians 3:13) I have learned by the word and by experience that victory is in the praise. We should not be alarmed when fiery trials come, we should give God praise. Think it not strange concerning your fiery trial as thou some strange things happened to you, but rejoice (Praise him) in as much as you are partakes of Christ sufferings. (1 Peter 4:12). It is becoming of the child of God to praise him in spite of the situation, circumstances. For Praise is comely for the upright (Psalms 32:1). The Bible says Praise the Lord O you servants of the Lord (Psalms 113:1). God desires all mankind to praise him let everything that have breath praise the Lord.(Psalms 150;6).

HE LAID DOWN HIS LIFE FOR ME SO THAT I COULD BE FREE

Jesus Christ declares that I am the good Shepherd and the good Shepherd gives his life for the sheep. (John 10:11) Before Jesus came down through 42 generations out of the root of Jesse (Isaiah 11:1). He wanted us to be free. Surely he borne our griefs and carried our sorrows. He did it because he want mankind to be free. We were a sheep that had gone astray and turned everyone to their own way, yet he Jesus) was wounded for our transgressions bruised for our iniquities, the chastisement of our peace was upon him and with his stripes we are healed. (Isaiah 53:5)- He sent his word for our freedom. He sent his word and his word healed them. (Psalms 107:20). His truth is designed for us to be free. You shall know the truth and the truth will make you free, therefore who the son sets free is free indeed. (John 8:32,33). Why did he do it when we were continually evil? (Genesis 6:5,6). Answer: God loves mankind. For God so loved the world that he gave his only begotten son that whoever believes on him should not perish but have everlasting life. (John 3:16). God commended (demonstrated) his love toward us in that while we were yet sinners Christ died for us (Romans 5:8)

TRICK OR TREAT

Sermon title: Trick or Treat- Our subject matter centers around 2 entities. One Tricks (Lies, schemes) The other Treats (Blesses, heals, etc.) The one that tricks is the devil. I admonish you to not let him trick you. The Bible says be sober (alert) be vigilant because your adversary (arch enemy of God) the devil walks about as a roaring lion seeking who he can devour. (1 Peter 5:8) He tricks through being a thief . The thief comes but for to steal, kill, and to destroy, thank God it's Jesus that Treats us for he said I am come that they might have life and life more abundantly. (John 10:10). We don't have to be taken in by the trickster God will treat us with Divine protection. They that dwell in the secret place of the most high shall abide under the shadow of the almighty. (Psalms 91:1). If you don't want to be tricked and you want to be treated. I say run in the name of the Lord. The name of the Lord is a strong tower the righteous run into it and they are safe. (Proverbs 18:10). The trickster is not greater than the treater. Greater is he that is within you than he that is in the world. (1 John 4:4). I know he tricks by throwing everything at you but the kitchen sink. Even if he throws the kitchen sink at you. There is no weapon formed against you that will prosper. (Isaiah 54:17). The song writer said don't let the devil RIDE he might want to DRIVE. Don't let him hold your HAND ✋HE MIGHT want to DANCE. Don't let him flag you DOWN he will put you on the GROUND!!

I Left The Light On

Sermon title: I left the light 💡on for you! Light symbolizes The love of Jesus Christ. He (Jesus) commended (demonstrated) his love toward us in that while we were yet sinners Christ died for us. (Romans 5:8). Light symbolizes his holiness. For it is written be you Holy (set apart by God) for I am Holy (set apart by God). (1 Peter 1:16). Jesus said as long as I am in the world I am the light of the world. (John 9:5). Now the spirit make the intercession for us with groaning which cannot be uttered. (Romans 8:26). In other words he has departed his earthly ministry, but he left the light on. How so Pastor? Answer: You are now the light of the world. (Matthew 5:14) He left the light on through you and I we are a city that is set on a hill that cannot be hid. Therefore because the light is left on. Jesus said let your light so shine before mankind, that they may see your good works. The light is left on not for us to be glorified and boast about ourselves but that they may glorify God who is in heaven. (Matthew 5:14-16). If someone doesn't value your worth don't let them cause you to dim your lights. If we walk in the light as he is in the light we have fellowship one with another and the blood of his son Jesus cleanse us from all unrighteousness. (1 John 1:7). I pray this message reaches the world 🌍the world in which God so loved, that he gave his only begotten son that whoever believes on him should not perish but have everlasting life. (John 3:16. The Gospel is the light that is left on for all mankind. Can't you hear Paul saying that I am not ashamed of the Gospel (Good news) for it is the power of God to everyone that belies to the Jew first and also to the Greeks. (Romans 1:16).

I Left The Light on Part 2

I left the light on PART 2- If we were on family feud hosted by Steve Harvey and he asked what are the top 5 reasons a person would leave the light on. Number 1 may be is that they are fearful. On the spiritual side of life we should be fearful if our lights are not turned on. The fear of the Lord is the beginning of knowledge. (Proverbs 1:7). David knew the light was left on. He said the Lord is my light and my salvation who shall I fear (Psalms 27:1). Can't you hear David saying yea thou I walk through the valley and the shadow of death I will fear no evil. (Psalms 23:1-5). Another reason one leave light on naturally is so they can see where they are going. Jesus said the Bible says if we say we have fellowship with him and walk in darkness, we lie and do not the truth. But if we walk in the light as he is in the light we have fellowship within and the blood of his son Jesus Christ cleanse us from our sin. For God is light and there is no darkness in him. (1 John 1:5-9). The devil has aim to bring us to darkness. Even in your selection of life and people we must realize that God has called us out of darkness into his marvelous light.1 Peter 2:9). Light and darkness are not in agreement (1 Corinthians 6:14). Therefore we should have no fellowship with the unfruitful works of darkness. (Ephesians 5:11).

BASIC INSTRUCTIONS
BEFORE LEAVING EARTH

Sermon Title:
Basic/Biblical
Instructions
Before
Leaving
Earth

Some have in life what they call a bucket 🧺 list. list of things they want to do/ accomplish before they leave earth. If we fail to complete everything we desire on this side, there are some basic/ biblical commands/ requirements given by God that it behaves us to get before we leave this earth or he returns.

1. Jesus said to Nicodemus that you must be born again. (John 3:5).

2. We must go to and through Jesus. Jesus said that without me you can do nothing. (John 15:5).

3. Jesus is all mankind access way to enter in. Jesus said I am the door (Access way) of the sheep (you and I) by me (Jesus) if anyone enters they shall be saved. (John 10:9).

4 Jesus is the only way to God the father. Jesus said to Thomas I am the way the truth and the life. No one comes to the father but by me. (John 14:6).

5 Salvation is only through Jesus. Neither is there salvation in any other for there is no other name under heaven given to men/mankind, whereby we must be saved (Acts 4:12).

AIM FOR IT AND GO AFTER THE PRIZE

In this life both spiritually and naturally Aim is an important factor in reaching/obtaining goals. We should Aim for the heavenly prize Aiming with our eyes 👀on the prize. David said I will lift my eyes 👀to the hills from where my help comes my help come from the Lord who made the heaven and earth. (Psalms 121:1). Paul taught in Hebrews to aim with our eyes but first said let us lay aside every weight and the sin which does so easily beset us. Looking (Aim) to Jesus the author and finisher of our faith. (Hebrews 12:2). To Aim for the prize our minds are very important. For so as on think 🗨, so are they. (Proverbs:23:7). Can't you hear Paul saying let this mind be in you which was also in Christ Jesus. (Philippians 2:5). Our Hearts are a key 🗝in going after the prize. Blessed are the pure in heart for they shall see God. (Matthew 5:8). Holiness (being set apart by God and for God) will get you the heavenly prize. Follow peace with all mankind, holiness without no one will see the Lord. (Hebrews 12:14.) Peter said be holy in all manner of conversation (Manner of life). Because it is written be you Holy for I am Holy (1 Peter 1:16).

NEVERTHELESS I WILL TAKE HIM AT HIS WORD PART 2

Part 2- Positive and prosperous things happen within our lives when we take him (Jesus) at his word. Jeremiah said is not my word like as a 🔥? and like a hammer ⛏that breaks the rock ☉in pieces? (Jeremiah 23:29). When he said I will not make mention of him or speak anymore in his name his word was in my heart as a burning fire 🔥shut up in my ╱ .(Jeremiah 20:9). David took him at his word and said his word is a lamp 🕎to my feet 👣and a light 💡to my pathway. (Psalms 119:105). Paul took him at his word and said the word of God is quick and powerful sharper than any two edged sword ⚔. (Hebrews 4:12). Peter took him at his word when Jesus told him to launch out into the deep and let down his net for a draught (Haul). Peter said Master we have toiled all night and have not caught anything. Nevertheless at your word I will let down the net for a draught (Haul). He caught so many the Bible says fishes 🐟🐟🐟🐟🐟🐟🐟🐟, their nets broke and they had to call for help. (Luke 5:4)

HE WILL MEET YOU WHERE YOU ARE AT AND TAKE YOU WHERE YOU NEED TO GO

Jesus Christ will meet us all where we are at. For Example David said I was sharpen in iniquity and in sin did my mother conceive me. (Psalms 51:5). Jesus came in the world to meet the sinners where they are at. This is a faithful saying and worthy of all acceptance, that Christ Jesus came into the world to save sinners (1 Timothy 1:15)He knew that we would get tired along the way, So he meets us where we are with words of encouragement. Let us not be weary in doing for we shall reap in due season if we faint not. (Galatians 6:9). He knew we might feel incomplete in life. He meets us where we are at with words of confidence. Being confident of this very thing that he (Jesus) who has begun a good work in you will perform (Complete)it until the day (coming) of Jesus Christ. (Philippians 1:6). Regardless of who you are or predicament you are in he will meet you where you are at. He that comes to me I will in no wise (case) cast him out. (John 6:37).

I GIVE YOU POWER & YOU SHOULD LIVE POWERFULLY

The power of God is given to mankind not so that we can use big exuberant words, he gives power that we may live powerful lives. Paul said my speech and my preaching was not with enticing words of man's wisdom but in demonstration of the spirit and power. (1 Corinthians 2:4). His power is not given based on social status or position in their community. He gives power to them that obey him. (Acts 5:32). When you walk in power Jesus who was made perfect became the author of eternal salvation unto all them that obey him. (Hebrews 5:9). In my closing I say that it takes his power within in order to live powerfully. Roman says if anyone doesn't have the spirit of Christ, he is none of his. (Romans 8:9). I want to be his and so do you therefore may it behoove us to be filled with his power. (John 3:5- You must be born again). Acts 1:8- After the Holy Ghost come upon you, you shall have power.) Acts 2:38- Repent of your sins every one of you and be baptized (Immersed in water) in the name (Authority, Character) of Jesus Christ for the remission of your sins and you shall receive the gift of the Holy Ghost.)

I GIVE YOU POWER
& YOU SHOULD LIVE
POWERFULLY PART 2

Part 2: Jesus Christ told us what his power would do to cause us to live powerful lives. He said believe (Have faith, rely, trust) on me as the scriptures have said and out of your belly (innermost) will flow rivers of living water. Speaking concerning his spirit for the Holy Ghost was not yet given. (John 7:38). He told the woman at the well, if you drink this water (natural water) you are going to thirst again. If you drink the water that I give you (Living water) you won't thirst no more for the water that I give you will be in you a well of water springing up into everlasting life. (John 4:14). We can/ should live powerfully. Jesus said you shall lay hands on the sick and they shall recover. (Mark 16:18). Jesus said to the 70 disciples (Followers/ learners) of God. Behold I give you power to tread upon serpents 🐍, and scorpions 🦂and over all the power of the enemy, and nothing by any means shall hurt you. (Luke 10:19). Having Power and not using it is like Jed Clampett having 40 million dollars 💵and eating possums for a delicatessen and bathing in a wash tub with lye soap. Nothing against eating possums if it be so but my point is eye hath not seen, nor ear heard neither has it entered into the heart of mankind the things the Lord has prepared for them that love him. (1 Corinthians 2:9).

LET HIM HAVE YOUR
BURDENS NOW

Two key words in our lesson text. One key word is LET (Allow) The other word is NOW (Not tomorrow, not when I get better) but right Now!! Jesus doesn't force himself upon any of us to take away our burdens. He said Let not (don't allow) your heart to be troubled. (John 14:1). He desires our minds to be like him but he won't make us do it. Let this mind 🖋 be in you that was also in him. (Philippians 2:5). He knows your load gets heavy and that your burdens are hard to bear. He says to you daughters come to me all who labor and are heavy laden and I will give you rest. (Matthew 11:28). We need not put off today for tomorrow. Today if you will hear his voice harden not your heart, behold today is the day of salvation and NOW is the acceptable time. (Hebrews 3:15). You that are struggling with habits I say to you let him have your burdens NOW!! Isaiah said to the people come NOW!! and LET us reason together (Let's talk it over) thou your sins be as scarlet they shall be white as snow ❄ thou they be red like crimson they shall be as wool. If you be willing and obedient you shall eat the good of the land. But if you refuse and rebel you will be devoured with the sword ⚔. The mouth of the Lord has spoken it. (Isaiah 1:18). Let him have your burdens now. Casting all your care upon him for he cares for you. (1 Peter 5:7).

REJECT THE PATTERNS OF THE WORLD AND RECEIVE THE PROMISES OF GOD PART 2

Part 2: In some form or facet we all should take inventory upon ourselves as to Rejecting the Patterns (Ways, mannerisms, lifestyle) of the world. We are to search the scriptures for in them Jesus said you think you have eternal life for these (those that have eternal life) are those who testify of me. (John 5:39). Bishop Edward L. Thomas taught us to wear the world lightly. Jesus gives us reason to. He says we are not of the world. If we were of the world the world would love his own. Because you are not of this world the world hates you. (John 15:19). As Bishop Ed Thomas would also say It's TIGHT but it's RIGHT!! We are to show the world that the promises of God are available, therefore we should put a difference between Holy and unholy, Between clean and unclean. (Leviticus 10:10). We don't reject it today and accept it tomorrow. No one can serve 2 masters either he will love the one and hate the other or he will hold to the one and despise the other. You cannot serve both God and Mammon (🔳🔳). We are to tell others of how he brought us out from the patterns of the world. Let the redeemed of the Lord say so whom he has redeemed from the hand of the enemy (Psalms 107:1). We are to show others that we have rejected the patterns of the world. Let your light so shine before men that they may see your good works and glorify our father who is in heaven. (Matthew 5:16)

I WON'T CHANGE MY STORY

When your story is a true story, be encouraged/determined to not change it (Don't make it different) Things have been tough lately, but don't change your story (The Joy of the Lord is still your strength).you have to cry 😢 sometimes, but don't change your story (They that sow in tears 😭, shall reap in Joy) Weeping May endure but a night, but Joy comes in the morning.

SATAN YOU CAN HUFF AND PUFF, BUT YOU CAN'T BLOW MY HOUSE DOWN

Satan is in similitude of the story in the 3 little pigs 🐷, he is huffing (being subtle and crafty,) and puffing (seeking who he can devour). I declare he cannot/ will not blow our house down (our bodies are described like a house 🏠) Know you not that your body is the temple of the Holy Ghost. The house Satan is huffing and puffing at is you. He is the thief that comes to steal, kill, and destroy, but he can't blow our house down, Jesus said I am come that you might have life and have it more abundantly. He desire to sift us as wheat 🌾, I heard Jesus tell Peter I have prayed for you that your faith does not fail you. He is as a roaring lion 🦁(notice as a roaring lion 🦁did not say he was a roaring lion 🦁) seeking who he can devour. He can't blow our house down when we cast all our care upon Him for He cares for us. We can stand on his promises the very gates of hell shall not prevail against us. No weapon formed against you shall prosper. Greater is he that is within you than he that is in the world.

THE END

Printed in the United States
by Baker & Taylor Publisher Services